TOWARD A
THREEFOLD
SOCIETY

Thinking – Feeling – Willing
Freedom – Equality – Fraternity

Rudolf Steiner

Translated by Frank Thomas Smith

Original Title in English:
Basic Issues of the Social Question

Original Title in German:
Die Kernpunkte der Sozialen Frage in den
Lebensnotwendigkeiten der Gegenwart und Zukunft
Dornach, Switzerland
(volume 23 in the Rudolf Steiner Bibliographical Survey,
1961).

Cover designed by
James D. Stewart, e.Librarian at the
Rudolf Steiner Archive & e.Lib
Visit the website at https://www.rsarchive.org/

Historical footnotes were prepared by the translator for
this English edition

Paperback: ISBN-13: 978-1-948302-16-6
Kindle: ISBN-13: 978-1-948302-17-3

Printed in the United States of America

"One can anticipate the experts who object to the complexity of these suggestions and find it uncomfortable even to think about three systems cooperating with each other, because they wish to know nothing of the real requirements of life and would structure everything according to the comfortable requirements of their own thinking. This must become clear to them: either people will accommodate their thinking to the requirements of reality, or they will have learned nothing from the calamity and will cause innumerable new ones to occur in the future."

— Rudolf Steiner

CONTENTS

Translator's Introduction vii

Preface to the Fourth German Edition — 1920 1

Preliminary Remarks 17

The True Nature of the Social Question 23

Finding Real Solutions to the Social Problems of the Times ... 49

Capitalism and Social Ideas 83

International Relations Between Social Organisms 133

To the German People and the Civilized World 153

About the Author 161

About the Translator 163

On-line Activities 165

Translator's Introduction

This book, *Basic issues of the Social Question* was written in 1919 for the German-speaking peoples of central Europe. It deals with the social problems of that time and suggests solutions. The question therefore arises: Is this book still relevant today, in the 21st century, for a worldwide readership?

In order to answer this question, let us first look at the book's very last paragraph: *One can anticipate the experts who object to the complexity of these suggestions and find it uncomfortable even to think about three systems cooperating with each other, because they wish to know nothing of the real requirements of life and would structure everything according to the comfortable requirements of their thinking. This must become clear to them: either people will accommodate their thinking to the requirements of reality, or they will have learned nothing from the calamity and will cause innumerable new ones to occur in the future.*

The calamity referred to is the First World War, and since that time history has certainly shown these words to be prophetic. Rudolf Steiner's suggestions were ignored in Central Europe at that time, at least by those who were in a position to put them into practice, and the calamities have been occurring 'innumerably' ever since. The 'social question' has not been resolved, nor have the steps been taken which are necessary to initiate the healing process. People all too often still look to the political state for the solution to all social problems, whether they be of an economic, spiritual (cultural), or political nature.

Where in the world is spiritual life, schools for example, free — not in the sense of cost, but free from state control and economic influence? Where does an 'associative' economy function? What political state is content with its legitimate function of ensuring that human rights are respected? The answer to all these questions is negative. The destructive tendencies which existed in 1919 are still very much with us; in fact, they have greatly increased their potency.

Certain historical circumstances are referred to, especially in Chapter Four, which were fresh in the minds of the readers in that part of the world at the time the book was written. Rudolf Steiner was born on 27 February 1861, in the town of Kraljevec, which was then in Austria-Hungary and is now in Croatia (he died on 30 March 1925 in Dornach, Switzerland), so the events relating to such political entities as the Austria-Hungarian and German empires were entirely familiar to him and, for the most part, to his readers. This is no longer the case, so I have added in-line 'Notes' within the text which can, however, only include a very brief description of the historical events referred to by the author.

In spite of the fact that certain descriptions refer to specific occurrences and attitudes of the times in which it was written, the suggestions and essential principles given by Rudolf Steiner are even more relevant today than when they were originally described, if only because their realization has since become even more urgent.

Frank Thomas Smith
October 2019

Preface to the Fourth German Edition – 1920

The challenges which contemporary society presents will be misunderstood by those who approach them with utopian ideas. It is of course possible to believe that any one of diverse theories, arrived at through personal observation and conviction, will result in making people happy. Such a belief can acquire overwhelming persuasive power. Nevertheless, as far as the social question of the times is concerned, it becomes irrelevant as soon as an attempt is made to assert it.

The following example, although seeming to carry this proposition to an extreme, is nevertheless valid. Let us assume that someone is in possession of a perfect, theoretical 'solution' to the social question. In spite of this, in attempting to offer it to the public he becomes the victim of an unpractical belief. We no longer live in an age in which public life can be influenced in this way. People's minds are simply not disposed to accept the ideas of another as far as this subject is concerned. They will not say: here is someone who knows how society should be structured, so we will act according to his opinions.

People are not interested in social ideas which are presented to them in this way. This book, which has already reached a fairly large audience, takes this phenomenon into consideration. Those who accuse it of having a utopian character have completely misunderstood my intentions. It is interesting to note that such criticism has come principally from people who themselves indulge almost exclusively in utopian thinking and are inclined to attribute their own mental habits to others.

Truly practical people know from experience that even the most convincing utopian ideas lead absolutely nowhere. In spite of this, many of them seem to feel obliged to propound just such ideas, especially in the field of economics. They should realize that they are wasting their breath, that their fellow men will not be able to apply such propositions.

The above should be treated as a fact of life inasmuch as it indicates an important characteristic of contemporary society, namely, that our present notions concerning economics, for example, have little relation to reality. How can we then hope to cope with the chaotic condition of society if we approach it with a thought process which has no relation to reality?

This question can hardly meet with favor as it requires the admission that our thinking is indeed remote from reality. Nevertheless, without such an admission we will not get to the bottom of the social question. Only when we understand that this divorce of thought from reality is a condition of the utmost seriousness for contemporary civilization, can we become clear in our own minds as to what society really needs.

The whole question revolves around the shape of contemporary spiritual life. Modern man has developed a spiritual life which is to a very large extent dependent upon political institutions and economic forces. While still a child he is given over to a state educational system, and his upbringing must correspond to the economic circumstances of his environment.

It is easy to believe that this situation results in the individual becoming well-adjusted to contemporary life, that the political state is best qualified to organize the educational system – and cultural affairs in general – for the benefit of the community. It is also easy to believe that the individual who is educated according to the economic conditions of his environment, and who is then placed according to these conditions becomes the best possible member of human society.

This book must assume the unpopular task of showing that the chaotic condition of our public life derives from the dependence of spiritual life on the political state and economic interests. It must also show that the liberation of spiritual life and culture from this dependence constitutes an important element of the burning social question.

This involves attacking certain wide-spread errors. For example, the political state's assumption of responsibility for education has long been considered to be beneficial for human progress. For people with socialistic ideas it is inconceivable that society should do anything but shape the individual according to its standards and for its service.

It is not easy to accept a very important fact of historical development, namely, that what was proper during an earlier period can be erroneous for a later period. For a new era in human relations to emerge, it was necessary that the circles which controlled education and culture be relieved of this function and that it be transferred to the political state. However, to persist in this arrangement is a grave social error.

The first part of this book attempts to indicate this. Human culture has matured toward freedom within the framework of the state, but it cannot exercise this freedom without complete autonomy of action. The nature which spiritual life has assumed requires that it constitute a fully autonomous member of the social organism. The administration of education, from which all culture develops, must be turned over to the educators. Economic and political considerations should be entirely excluded from this administration. Each teacher should arrange his or her time so that they can also be an administrator in their field. They should be just as much at home attending to administrative matters as they are in the classroom. No one should make decisions who is not directly engaged in the educational process. No parliament or congress, nor any individual who was perhaps once an educator, is to have anything to say. What is experienced in the teaching process would then flow naturally into the administration. By its very nature such a system would engender competence and objectivity.

Of course, one could object that such a self-governing spiritual-cultural sector would not be perfect either. But we cannot expect perfection; we can only strive toward the best possible situation. The capabilities which the child develops can best be transmitted to the community if its education is the exclusive responsibility of those whose judgment rests on a spiritual foundation. To what extent a child should be taught one thing or another, can only be correctly determined within a free cultural community. How such determinations are to be made binding is also a matter for this community. The state and the economy would be able to absorb vigor from such a community, which is not attainable when the organization of cultural institutions is based on political and economic standards.

Even the schools which directly serve the state and the economy should be administered by the educators: law schools, trade-schools, agricultural and industrial colleges, all should be administered by the representatives of a free spiritual life. This book will necessarily arouse many prejudices, especially if the consequences of its thesis are considered. What is the source of these prejudices? We recognize their antisocial nature when we perceive that they originate in the unconscious belief that teachers are impractical people who cannot be trusted to assume practical responsibilities on their own. It is assumed that all organization must be carried out by those who are engaged in practical matters, and educators should act according to the terms of reference determined for them.

This assumption ignores the fact that it is just when teachers are not permitted to determine their own functions that they tend to become impractical and remote from reality. As long as the so-called experts determine the terms of reference according to which they must function, they will never be in a position to turn out practical individuals who are equipped for life by their education. The current antisocial state of affairs is the result of individuals entering society who lack social sensitivity because of their education. Socially sensitive individuals can only develop within an educational system which is conducted and administered by other socially sensitive individuals. No progress will be made towards solving the social question if we do not treat the question of education and culture as an essential part of it. An antisocial situation is not merely the result of economic structures, it is also caused by the antisocial behavior of the individuals who are active in these structures. It is antisocial to allow youth to be educated by people who themselves have become strangers to reality because the conduct and content of their work has been dictated to them from without.

The state establishes law schools and requires that the law they teach be in accordance with the state's own view of jurisprudence. If these schools were established as free cultural institutions, they would derive the substance of their jurisprudence from this very culture. The state would then become the recipient of what this free spiritual life has to offer. It would be enriched by the living ideas which can only arise within such a spiritual environment. Within a spiritual life of this nature society would encounter the men and women who could grow into it on their own terms. Worldliness does not originate in educational institutions organized by so-called 'experts,' in which impractical people teach, but only in educators who understand life and the world according to their own viewpoints. Particulars of how such a free culture should organize itself are outlined in this book.

The utopian-minded will approach the book with all kinds of doubts. Anxious artists and other spiritual workers will question whether talent would be better off in a free culture than in one which is provided for by the state and economic interests, as is the case today. Such doubters should bear in mind that this book is not meant to be the least bit utopian. No hard and fast theories are found in it which say that things must be this way or that. On the contrary, its intention is to stimulate the formation of communities which, as a result of their common experience, will be able to bring about what is socially desirable. If we consider life from experience instead of theoretical preconceptions, we will agree that creative individuals would have better prospects of seeing their work fairly judged if a free cultural community existed which could act according to its own values.

The 'social question' is not something which has suddenly appeared at this stage of human evolution and which can be resolved by a few individuals or by some parliamentary body and stay resolved. It is an integral part of modern civilization which has come to stay, and as such will have to be resolved anew for each moment in the world's historical development. Humanity has now entered into a phase in which social institutions constantly produce antisocial tendencies. These tendencies must be overcome each time. Just as a satiated organism experiences hunger again after a period of time, so the social organism passes from order to disorder. A food which permanently stills hunger does not exist; neither does a universal social panacea. Nevertheless, people can enter into communities in which they would be able to continuously direct their activities in a social direction. One such community is the self-governing spiritual/cultural branch of the social organism.

Observation of the contemporary world indicates that the spiritual/cultural sector requires free self-administration, while the economy requires associative work. The modern economic process consists of the production, circulation and consumption of commodities. Human needs are satisfied by means of this process and human beings are directly involved in it, each having his own part-interest, each participating to the extent he is able. What each individual really needs can only be known by himself, what he should contribute he can determine through his insight into the situation as a whole. It was not always so, and it is not yet the case the world over; but it is essentially true as far as the civilized inhabitants of the earth are concerned.

Economic activity has expanded in the course of human evolution. Town economies developed from closed household economies and in turn grew into national economies. Today we stand before a global economy. Undoubtedly the new contains much of the old, just as the old showed indications of what was to come. Nevertheless, human destiny is conditioned by the fact that this process, in most fields of economic endeavor, has already been accomplished. Any attempt to organize economic forces into an abstract world community is erroneous. In the course of evolution private economic enterprise has, to a large extent, become state economic enterprise. But the political states are not merely the products of economic forces, and the attempt to transform them into economic communities is the cause of the social chaos of modern times. Economic life is striving to structure itself according to its own nature, independent of political institutionalization and mentality. It can only do this if associations, comprised of consumers, distributors and producers, are established according to purely economic criteria. Actual conditions would determine the scope of these associations. If they are too small, they would be too costly; if they are too large, they would become economically unmanageable. Practical necessity would indicate how inter-associational relations should develop. There is no need to fear that individual mobility would be inhibited due to the existence of associations. He who requires mobility would experience flexibility in passing from one association to another, as long as economic interest and not political organization determines the move. It is possible to foresee processes within such associations which are comparable to currency in circulation.

Professionalism and objectivity could cause a general harmony of interests to prevail in the associations. Not laws, but people using their immediate insights and interests, would regulate the production, circulation and consumption of goods. They would acquire the necessary insights through their participation in the associations; goods could circulate at their appropriate values due to the fact that the various interests represented would be compensated by means of contracts. This type of economic cooperation is quite different from that practiced by the labor-unions which, although operational in the economic field, are established according to political instead of economic principles. Basically, parliamentary bodies, they do not function according to economic principles of reciprocal output. But in the associations, there would be no 'wage earners' using their collective strength to demand the highest possible wages from management, but artisans who, together with management and consumer representatives, determine reciprocal outputs by means of price regulation – something which cannot be accomplished by sessions of parliamentary bodies. This is important! For who would do the work if countless man-hours were spent in negotiations about it? But with person to person, association to association agreements, work would go on as usual. Of course, it is necessary that all agreements reflect the workers' insights and the consumers' interests. This is not the description of a utopia. I am not saying how things should be arranged but indicating how people will arrange things for themselves once they activate the type of associative communities which correspond to their own insights and interests.

Human nature would see to it that men and women unite in such economic communities, were they not prevented from doing so by political state intervention, for nature determines needs. A free spiritual life would also contribute, for it begets social insights. Anyone who is in a position to consider all this from experience will have to admit that these economic associations could come into being at any moment, and that there is nothing utopian about them. All that stands in their way is modern man's obsession with the external organization of economic activity. Free association is the exact opposite of this external organizing for the purpose of production. When people associate, the planning of the whole originates in the reasoning of the individual. What is the point of those who own no property associating with those who do! It may seem preferable to 'justly' regulate production and consumption externally. Such external planning sacrifices the free, creative initiative of the individual, thereby depriving the economy of what such initiative alone can give it. If, in spite of all prejudice, an attempt were made today to establish such associations, the reciprocal output between owners and non-owners would necessarily occur. The instincts which govern the consideration of such things nowadays do not originate in economic experience, but in sentiments which have developed from class and other interests. They were able to develop because purely economic thought has not kept pace with the complexities of modern economics. An unfree spiritual-culture has prevented this. The individuals who labor in industry are caught in a routine, and the formative economic forces are invisible to them. They labor without having insight into the wholeness of human life. In the associations each individual would learn what he should know through contact with others. Through the participants' insight and experience in relation to their respective activities and their resulting ability to exercise collective judgment, knowledge of what is economically possible would arise. In a free spiritual life, the only active forces are those inherent in it; in the same sense, the only economic values active in an associatively structured economic system would be those which develop through the associations themselves. The individual's role would emerge from cooperation with his associates. He could thereby exert just as much economic influence as corresponds to his output. How the non-productive elements would be integrated into economic life will be explained in the course of the book. Only an economic system which is self-structured can protect the weak against the strong.

We have seen that the social organism can be arranged into two autonomous members able to support each other only because each is self-governing according to its inherent nature. Between them a third element must function: the political state. Here is where each individual who is of age can make his influence and judgment felt. In free spiritual life each person works according to his particular abilities; in the economic sphere each takes his place according to his associative relationship. In the context of the political rights-state the purely human element comes into its own, insofar as it is independent of the abilities by means of which the individual is active in spiritual/cultural life, and independent of the value accrued to the goods he produces in the associative economic sphere.

I have attempted to show in this book how hours and conditions of labor are matters to be dealt with by the political rights-state. All are equal in this area due to the fact that only matters are to be treated in it about which all are equally competent to form an opinion.

Human rights and obligations are to be determined within this member of the social organism.

The unity of the whole social organism will originate in the independent development of its three members. The book will show how the effectiveness of capital, means of production and land use, can be determined through the cooperation of the three members or sectors. Those who wish to solve the social question by means of some economic scheme will find this book impractical. However, those who have practical experience and would stimulate men and women to cooperative ventures through which they can best recognize and dedicate themselves to the social tasks of the day, will perhaps not deny that the author is in fact advocating something which is in accordance with the practical facts of life.

This book was first published in 1919. As a supplement I published various articles in the magazine "Dreigliederung des Sozialen Organismus," which subsequently appeared as a separate volume with the title, *In Ausführung der Dreigliederung des Sozialen Organismus*[1]. In both of these publications much more

---

[1] *In Ausführung der Dreigliederung des Sozialen Organismus*. These 22 essays by Rudolf Steiner, along with 44 others on the subject, are now contained in a volume entitled *Aufsätze über die Dreigliederung des Sozialen Organismus* (Essays on the Triformation of the Social Organism) published in 1961 by the Rudolf Steiner Verlag, Dornach, Switzerland.

emphasis is placed on the means which should be employed than on the ends, or 'objectives' of the social movement. If we think realistically, we know that particular ends appear in diverse forms. Only when we think in abstractions does everything appear to us in clearly defined outlines. The abstract thinker will often reproach the practical realist for lack of distinctness, for not being sufficiently 'clear' in his presentations. Often those who consider themselves to be experts are, in reality, just such abstractionists. They do not realize that life can assume the most varied forms. It is a flowing element, and if we wish to move with it we must adapt our thoughts and feelings to this flowing characteristic. Social tasks can be grasped with this type of thinking. The ideas presented in this book have been drawn from an observation of life; an understanding of them can be derived from the same source.

Preliminary Remarks

The contemporary social situation poses grave and comprehensive challenges. The demands which have arisen for new structures indicate that the solutions to these challenges must be sought in ways which have not been previously considered. Conditions being what they are, the time has perhaps come when attention will be paid to someone whose experience in life obliges him to contend that thoughtlessness concerning the ways which have become necessary has resulted in social chaos. The arguments presented in this book are based on this opinion. They deal with the prerequisites for transforming the demands of a large part of contemporary humanity into purposeful social will. The formation of this will should not depend on whether the demands please some of us or not. They exist and must be dealt with as social facts. This should be kept in mind by those whose position in life causes them to find distasteful the author's description of proletarian demands as something which must be reconciled by social will. The author wishes to speak only in accordance with the realities of contemporary life, insofar as his experience enables him to do so. He has seen the inevitable consequences of ignoring the facts which have unfolded in the life of modern man and of being blind to the necessity of a social will to deal with them.

Self-styled experts in practical matters (what have come to be regarded as practical matters under the influence of routine) will, at first, be dissatisfied with the arguments presented in this book. But it is just such persons as these who should undergo a relearning process, for their 'expertise' has been proven by recent events to be absolutely erroneous and has led to disastrous consequences. They must learn to recognize many things as practical which have seemed to them to be eccentric idealism. They may be critical of the fact that the early parts of the book deal more with the spiritual life of modern humanity than with economics. The author is obliged however, from his personal knowledge of life, to take the position that the errors of the past will only multiply if the decision is not made to focus attention on modern humanity's spiritual life. Equally dissatisfied with what the author says in this book will be those who are continuously intoning clichés about mankind abandoning purely materialistic interests and turning to 'the spirit,' to 'idealism,' for he attaches little importance to the mere reference to 'the spirit' and talk about a nebulous spiritual world. He can only recognize a spirituality which constitutes the living substance of humanity. This manifests itself in the mastery of practical aspects as well as in the formulation of a worldview and of life which is capable of satisfying the needs of the soul. It is not a matter of knowing — or believing to know — about spirituality, but that it be a spirituality which is also applicable to the practical realities of everyday life, one which accompanies these everyday realities and is not a mere sideline reserved for the inner life of the soul. To the 'spiritualists' the arguments presented in this book will be too unspiritual, while to the 'practical' ones they will seem unrealistic. The author is of the opinion, however, that he may be useful to contemporary society in his way just because he does not share the impracticality of those persons who consider themselves to be practical, nor can he find any justification for the kind of talk about the 'spirit' that results in illusions.

The social question is spoken of in this book as an economic, a human rights and a spiritual-cultural question. The author is convinced that the true nature of this question reveals itself in the requirements of the economic, rights and spiritual-cultural spheres of society. The impulse for a healthy coordination of these three spheres within the social organism can emerge from a recognition of this fact. During previous periods of human evolution social instincts saw to it that the three areas were integrated in society in a way which corresponded to human nature as it was then. At the present however, it is necessary for mankind to structure society by means of purposeful social will. Between those past epochs and the present there is a confusion of old instincts and modern consciousness which is no longer competent to deal with the demands of modern humanity, at least as far as those countries are concerned in which such a will is meaningful. Often the old instincts persist in what passes today for purposeful social thinking. This weakens thinking in relation to the tasks it must face. A more profound effort than has been hitherto supposed must be made by the men and women of the present in order to work their way free of what is no longer viable. How the economic, rights and spiritual spheres are to be structured in a way which corresponds to the demands of modern society can, in my opinion, only be determined if sufficient good will is developed to recognize this fact. What I believe is necessary concerning the shape such structures should take is submitted to contemporary judgment by means of this book. My wish is to provide a stimulus along a way which leads to social objectives that correspond to contemporary realities and necessities. For I believe that only such efforts can transcend emotions and utopias where social will is concerned.

If, in spite of this, some readers find elements of this book utopian, then the author would suggest they consider how often ideas concerning possible social developments are so completely divorced from reality that they degenerate into nonsense. For this reason, one is inclined to find utopias even in arguments which derive from reality and direct experience, as has been attempted in this book. One sees an argument as 'abstract' because only the habitual is 'concrete,' and the concrete is abstract if it does not coincide with the habitual manner of thinking.*

I realize that followers of strict party programs will at first be unhappy with this book. Nevertheless, I am confident that many political party members will soon come to the conclusion that events have already far outstripped party programs and that a determination, independent of such programs, concerning the immediate objectives of social will is necessary.

April 1919,

Rudolf Steiner

[* I have purposely avoided confining myself to the customary political economic terminology. I know exactly which passages a 'specialist' opinion will call amateurish. My form of expression was determined not only by my desire to address myself also to people who are not familiar with political and social scientific literature, but primarily because of my view that a new age will judge most of what is specialized in this literature, including its terminology. to be one-sided and inadequate. I would remind those who feel that I should have referred to seemingly similar social ideas of others, that the points of departure and the ways described here, for which I can thank decades of experience, are the essential points towards a practical realization of the given impulses, and not merely this or that type of thinking. Furthermore, as can be gathered from Chapter Four. I had already committed myself to an attempt at practical realization, when seemingly similar ideas in respect to one point or another had not yet been noticed.]

Chapter One

The True Nature of the Social Question

Does not the catastrophe of the World War demonstrate the deficiency of the thinking which for decades was supposed to have understood the will of the proletariat? Does not the true nature of the social movement stand revealed by the fact of this catastrophe?

It is necessary to ask these questions, for the demands of the proletariat, previously suppressed, are surging to the surface now that the powers of suppression have been partially destroyed. But to maintain the position which these powers took in relation to the social urges of a large part of humanity is something which can only be desired by someone totally ignorant of the indestructibility of such impulses in human nature.

Many of the key people who were able to influence the European powers which in 1914 were intent on rushing headlong into the catastrophe of war were victims of a great illusion in respect to these impulses. They actually believed that a military victory for their side would still the impending social storm. They have since had to admit that their own behavior gave the social urges the impetus they were waiting for. Indeed, the present human catastrophe has revealed itself to be the historical event through which these urges attained to their full driving force.

During these last fateful years, the leading persons and classes have had to condition their behavior to the attitudes of the socialist circles, although if it had been possible to ignore them, they would gladly have done so. The form events have since taken is the result of these attitudes. Now that a decisive stage — in preparation for decades — has been reached, a tragedy unfolds because thinking has not kept pace with events. Many people who have been trained to think in terms of developments in which they saw social ideals are now helpless when confronted with the grave problems which the facts present.

Some still believe that their ideas concerning a restructuring of society will somehow be realized and prove sufficiently efficacious to guide events in a positive direction. The deluded opinion that the old scheme of things should be retained in spite of the demands of a majority of mankind can be dismissed off-hand, and attention should be shifted to those who are convinced of the necessity for social renewal. In any case, we are obliged to admit that party platforms drift around among us like so many mummified ideas which are continuously refuted by the facts. These facts require decisions for which party programs are unprepared. The political parties have evolved along with events but have fallen behind in respect of their thinking habits. It is perhaps not presumptuous to maintain that these conclusions — which are contrary to what is generally believed — can be properly arrived at through a correct appraisal of contemporary events. It is possible to deduce from this that the times should be receptive to a characterization of the social life of humanity which, in its originality, is foreign to the thinking of most socially oriented personages as well as to party platforms. It is quite possible that the tragedy of the attempts to solve the social question is attributable to a misunderstanding of the meaning of the proletarian struggle, even on the part of those whose ideas have originated in that struggle. For people are by no means always able to derive correct judgments from their own desires.

It would therefore appear justified to ask the following questions: What does the modern proletarian movement really want? – and does this correspond to what is generally considered to be its objective by the non-proletariat and the proletariat alike? Does the true nature of the social question agree with what is commonly thought about it, or is a completely different way of thinking necessary? This question can hardly be answered objectively except by one who has been in a practical position to understand the modern proletarian mind, especially the minds of those members of the proletariat who have been instrumental in determining the direction which the social movement has taken.

Much has been said about the development of modern technology and capitalism, the birth of a new proletarian working class, and how its demands have arisen within the new economic system. Much of what has been said is relevant, but that nothing decisive has been touched upon is evident to anyone who has not been hypnotized by the idea that external conditions determine the nature of human life, and who is objectively aware of the impulses which originate in the human soul. It is true that the demands of the proletariat have arisen during the evolution of modern technology and capitalism, but recognition of this fact says nothing about the purely human impulse residing in these demands. As long as these impulses are not fully understood, the true nature of the 'social question' will remain inscrutable.

The significance of the following expression is apparent to anyone who has become familiar with the deep-seated, internal forces of the human will: the modern worker has become class-conscious. He no longer instinctively follows the lead of the other social classes; he considers himself to be a member of a separate class and is determined to influence the relations between his class and the others in a manner which will be advantageous to his own interests. The psychological undercurrents related to the expression 'class conscious,' as used by the modern proletariat, provide an insight into the mentality of a working class which is bound up with modern technology and capitalism. It is important to recognize the profound impression which scientific teachings about economics and its influence on human destiny have made on the mind of the proletarian. Here a fact is touched upon concerning which many people who can only think *about* the proletarian and not *with* him have murky, if not downright dangerous notions, considering the seriousness of contemporary events. The opinion that the 'uncultivated' worker has been deceived by Marxism and the proletarian writers who promulgate it, is not conducive to an understanding of the historical situation. This opinion reveals a lack of insight into an essential element of the social movement: that the proletarian class consciousness has been cultivated by concepts which derive from modern scientific developments. The sentiment expressed in Ferdinand Lassalle's[2] speech 'Science and the Worker' continues to

---

[2] Ferdinand Lassalle. 1825-1864, founder of the Social Democratic movement in Germany. The speech referred to here was made before the Berlin criminal court 'in defense against the charge of having publicly incited the property-less classes to hate and contempt

dominate this consciousness. This may seem unimportant to certain 'practical' people. Nevertheless, a truly effective insight into the modern labor movement requires that attention be focused on this subject. What both the moderate and radical wings of the proletarian movement are demanding reflects the economic science which has captivated their imagination and not, as has been maintained, economic life itself somehow transformed into a human impulse. This is clearly illustrated by the popularized scientific character of proletarian literature; to deny it is to shut one's eyes to the facts. A fundamental, determining characteristic of the present social situation is that the modern proletarian is able to define the content of his class consciousness in scientifically oriented concepts. The working man at his machine may be far removed from 'science' as such; nevertheless, he hears the explanation of his situation from others whose knowledge is derived from this science.

All the discussion about the new economics, the machine age, capitalism, etc., may be most enlightening in respect to the underlying causes of the proletarian movement. However, the determining factor of the present social situation is not that the worker has been harnessed to a machine within the capitalistic system, but that certain thoughts, influenced by his dependent

of the property owners,' on 16 January, 1863. Ferdinand Lassalle Gesammelte Reden und Schriften. Berlin 1919/20.

position within the capitalistic world order, have developed in his class consciousness. It may be that the present habits of thought inhibit recognition of the implications of this fact and make it appear that to emphasize it constitutes no more than a dialectic game of concepts. This must be answered as follows: there is no prospect of a successful intervention in modern society without comprehension of the essential elements involved. Anyone who wishes to understand the proletarian movement must first of all know how the proletarian thinks. For this movement – from its moderate efforts at reform to its most excessive abuses – is not activated by 'non-human forces' or 'economic impulses,' but by people, by their ideas and by their will.

The decisive ideas and forces of will of the contemporary social movement are not contained in what technology and capitalism have implanted in the proletarian consciousness. The movement has turned to modern science for the source of its ideas, because technology and capitalism were not able to provide the worker with the human dignity his soul needed. This dignity was available to the medieval artisan through his craft, to which he felt humanly related; a situation which allowed him to consider life in society as worth living. He was able to view what he was doing as the realization of his striving as a human being. Under capitalism and technology, however, he had no recourse but himself, his own inner being, in seeking the basis for an understanding of what a human being is; for this basis is not contained in capitalism and technology. Therefore, the proletarian consciousness chose the path of scientifically oriented thinking. The inherently human element of society had been lost. This happened at a time when the leading classes were cultivating a scientific mode of thinking which no longer possessed the spiritual impact necessary to satisfy the manifold needs of an expanding human consciousness. The old worldviews considered the human being to be a soul-entity existing within a spiritually existential framework. According to modern scientific thought, however, he is no more than a natural being within the natural order of things. This science is not experienced as a current which flows into man's mind from a spiritual world which also sustains his soul. An impartial consideration of history reveals that scientific ideation has evolved from religious ideation. This must be admitted in spite of how one may feel about the relationship between the various religious impulses and modern scientific thinking. But these old worldviews, with their religious foundations, were not able to impart their soul-sustaining impulses to modern modes of thinking. They withdrew and tried to exist outside these modes of thinking at a consciousness level which the proletarian mind found inaccessible. This level of consciousness was still of some value to the members of the ruling classes, as it more or less corresponded to their social position.

These classes sought no new conceptions because tradition enabled them to retain the old. But the worker, stripped of his traditions, found his life completely transformed. Deprived of the old ways, he lost the ability to take sustenance from spiritual sources, from which he had also been alienated. Broadly speaking, modern scientism developed simultaneously with technology and capitalism, attracting in the process the faith and confidence of the modern proletariat in search of a new consciousness and new values. But the workers acquired a different relationship to scientism than did the members of the ruling classes, who did not feel the need to adapt their own psychological needs to the new scientific outlook. In spite of being thoroughly imbued with the scientific conception of causal relationships leading from the lowest animal up to man, it remained for them a purely theoretical conviction; they did not feel the necessity to restructure their lives according to this conviction. The naturalist Vogt and the popular science writer Büchner, for example, were certainly imbued with the scientific outlook. Alongside this outlook, however, something was active in their souls which enabled them to retain certain attitudes in life which can only be justified through belief in a universal, spiritual order of things. How differently scientism affects someone whose life is firmly grounded in such circumstances and the modern proletarian who is continuously harangued by agitators during his few free hours with such things as: *modern science has cured man of believing that he has a spiritual origin;* he knows now that in primitive times he clambered indecorously around in trees and that he has a purely natural origin. The modern proletarian found himself confronted with such ideas whenever he sought a psychological foundation which would permit him to find his place in the scheme of things. He became deadly serious about the new scientism and drew from it his own conclusions about life. The technological, capitalistic age affected him quite differently than it did the ruling classes, whose way of life was still supported by spiritually rewarding impulses; it was in their interest to adapt the accomplishments of the new age to this life-style. The proletarian however, had been deprived of his old way of life which, in any case, was no longer capable of providing him with a sense of his value as a human being. The only thing which seemed capable of providing the answer to the question: What is a human being? — was the new scientific outlook, equipped as it was with the powers of faith derived from the old ways.

It is of course possible to be amused at the description of the proletarian's manner of thinking as 'scientific'; but only by equating science with what is acquired through years of attendance at 'institutes of higher learning,' and by contrasting it to the consciousness of the proletarian, who is 'unlearned.' Such amusement ignores one of the decisive facts of contemporary life, namely that many a highly educated person lives unscientifically, while the unlearned proletarian orients his entire way of life according to a science which he perhaps does not even possess. The educated person has taken science and pigeon-holed it in a compartment of his mind, but his sentiments are determined by societal relations which do not depend on this science. The proletarian, however, is obliged by his circumstances to experience existence in a way which corresponds to scientific convictions. His level of knowledge may well be far removed from what the other classes call 'scientific'; his life is nevertheless oriented by scientific ideation. The life-style of the other classes is determined by a religious, an aesthetic, a general cultural foundation; but for him 'science,' down to its most insignificant details, has become dogma. Many members of the leading classes consider themselves to be 'enlightened,' 'free-thinking.' Scientific conviction certainly lives in their intellects, but their hearts still pulse with unconscious vestiges of traditional beliefs.

What the old ways did not transmit to the scientific outlook was the awareness of a spiritual origin. The members of the ruling classes could afford to disregard this characteristic of modern scientism because their lives were still determined by tradition. The members of the proletariat could not. Tradition had been driven from their souls by their new position in society. They inherited the scientific outlook from the ruling classes and turned it into the basis for a conception of the essence of man, a conception which was ignorant of its own spiritual origin; which, in fact, denied any such spiritual origin.

I am well aware of what effect these ideas will have on non-members of the proletariat and members alike, who feel themselves to be practical people, and who consequently consider what has been said here to be remote from reality. But the facts which are emerging from the world situation will eventually prove this opinion erroneous. An objective consideration of these facts reveals that a superficial interpretation of life only has access to ideas which no longer coincide with the facts. Prevailing thought has been 'practical' for so long that it has not the slightest relationship to the facts. The present catastrophic world situation could be a lesson for many: what did they think would happen, and what did happen? Must this also be the case with social thinking?

I can also imagine the reproach of someone who professes the proletarian viewpoint: 'Another one who would like to divert the basic issues of the social question on to paths which are amenable to the bourgeoisie.' Such a person does not realize that, although destiny has placed him in a proletarian milieu, his mode of thinking has been inherited from the ruling classes. He lives proletarian, but he thinks bourgeois. The new times do not only require a new way of life, but also a new way of thinking. The scientific outlook will become life sustaining only if its manner of dealing with the question of a fully human attitude to life attains to a force equal to that which animated the old ideas.

A path is herewith indicated which leads to the discovery of one element of the modern proletarian movement. At the end of this path a conviction is intoned in the proletarian mind: 'I seek a spiritual life. But spiritual life is an ideology, a reflection in people of outward occurrences which does not originate in a spiritual world.' What has emerged in modern times in the transition from the old cultural-spiritual life is regarded by the proletariat as ideology. In order to capture the mood of the proletarian mind as it manifests itself in social demands, it is necessary to realize what effect the view that spiritual life is an ideology can have. It is possible to object that the average worker knows nothing of this view, that it more likely addles the half-educated minds of his leaders. To hold this opinion is to be ignorant of the facts, is to be unaware of what has taken place in the lives of the working classes during the last decades, is to be blind to the relationship which exists between the view that spiritual life is an ideology, the demands and deeds of the so-called 'ignorant' radical socialists and the acts of those who hatch revolutions out of obscure impulses.

It is tragic that there is so little empathy for the emerging mood of the masses and for what is really taking place in people's minds. The non-proletarian listens with anxiety to the demands of the proletariat and hears the following: 'Only through socialization of the means of production is it possible for me to attain to a dignified human existence.' What he does not realize is that his class, in the transition from the old times to the new, has not only set the proletarian to work at means of production which are not his, it has also failed to provide him with nourishment for his soul. People who think in the way described above may claim that the worker simply wants to attain to the same standard of living which the ruling classes possess, and they will ask what this has to do with his soul. Even the worker may contend that he claims nothing from the other classes for his soul, that he only wants them to stop exploiting him and that class differences cease to exist. Such talk does not reach the essence of the social question, reveals nothing of its true nature. For had the working people inherited a genuine spiritual content from the ruling classes, and not one which considers spiritual life to be an ideology, then its social demands would have been presented quite differently. The proletarian is convinced of the ideological nature of spiritual life but becomes steadily unhappier as the result of this conviction. The effects of this unconscious misery, from which he suffers acutely, outweigh by far in importance for the present social situation the justified demands for an improvement in external conditions.

The members of the ruling classes do not recognize themselves as the authors of the militancy which confronts them from the proletarian world. But they are the authors in that they have bequeathed to the proletariat a spiritual life which is bound to be considered an ideology.

The social movement is not characterized by the demand for a change in the living standards of a particular social class, but rather by how the demand for this change is translated into reality by means of the thinking of this class. Let us consider the facts for a moment from this point of view. We will see how those persons who like to think along proletarian lines smile at the contention that any spiritual endeavor could possibly contribute toward solving the social question. They dismiss it as ideology, as abstract theory. They think that no meaningful solutions to the burning social questions of the day can come from mere ideas, from a so-called spiritual life. But upon closer examination it becomes obvious that the nerve center, the fundamental impulse of the modern proletarian movement, does not reside in what the proletarian talks about, but in ideas.

The proletarian movement is – to an extent perhaps unequaled by any similar movement in history – a movement born of ideas. The more closely it is studied, the more emphatically is this seen to be true. This conclusion has not been arrived at lightly. For years I taught a wide range of subjects in a workers' educational institute[3]. Through this experience I have come to recognize what is alive and striving in the modern proletarian worker's soul. I was also able to observe the activities of the various labor and trade unions. I feel, therefore, that I do not base myself on mere theoretical considerations, but on the results of actual experience.

To know the modern workers' movement where it is being carried out by workers (unfortunately, this is seldom the case as far as the leading intellectuals are concerned) is to recognize the profound significance of the fact that a certain trend of thought has captured the minds of an exceedingly large number of people in an extremely intensive way. The fact that the social classes are so antagonistic to each other makes the formulation of a position regarding social problems quite difficult. The middle classes of today find it very difficult to identify with the working class and cannot therefore understand how such an intellectually demanding

---

[3] Rudolf Steiner taught history and science subjects in the Workers' Training School in Berlin, a socialistically oriented institution, from 1899 to 1904. See chapter 28 of his autobiography, *The Course of my Life*. Although his courses were very popular with the worker-students, he was eventually forced to leave because the content of his teaching was neither materialistic nor Marxist.

dialectic as that of Karl Marx – regardless of what one may think of its content – could have found receptivity in the virgin proletarian intelligence.

Karl Marx's system of thought can be accepted by one individual and rejected by another, perhaps with reasons which appear to be equally valid. It was even revised after the death of Marx and his friend Engels by those who saw society from a somewhat different viewpoint. I do not wish to discuss here the content of this system, which is not, in my opinion, the meaningful element in the modern proletarian movement. Its most meaningful characteristic is, to me, the fact that the most powerful impulse active in the working-class world is a system of thought. No practical movement with such fundamental, everyday demands has ever stood so exclusively on a foundation of pure ideation as does this modern proletarian movement. It is the first movement of its kind in history to have chosen a scientific foundation. This fact must be properly understood. What the modern proletarian consciously has to say, program-wise, about his own opinions, his wants and his feelings, does not seem to be essential.

Most important is that the intellectual foundation for life affects the whole man, whereas the other classes restrict it to particular compartments of the mind. The proletarian is unable to acknowledge this process because the realm of intellect, of thought, has been bequeathed to him as an ideology. In reality he builds his life on ideas, which at the same time he considers to be unreal ideology. It is not possible to understand the proletarian interpretation of life and its realization through the acts of its adherents without also comprehending this fact and its consequences for human evolution.

It follows from what has been expounded above that any description of the true nature of the proletarian social movement must give priority to a description of the modern worker's spiritual life. It is essential that the worker sense the causes of his unsatisfactory social situation and encounter the methods for changing it in this same spiritual life. Nevertheless, at present he is not yet able to do anything except angrily or contemptuously reject the contention that a meaningful impellent resides in these spiritual undercurrents of the social movement. How is he to recognize an impellent, which affects himself, in what he must consider to be an ideology? One cannot expect to resolve an untenable social situation by means of a spiritual life so perceived. Due to a scientifically oriented point of view not only science itself, but also art, religion, morality and justice are considered to be facets of human ideology by the modern proletarian. He sees in these aspects of spiritual life nothing that relates to the reality of his existence and which could contribute to his material well-being. To him they are a mere reflection of the material life.

Although they may indirectly react upon man's material life through the intellect or by influencing will impulses, they originally arose as ideological emanations of this same material life. He feels that they cannot contribute to the solution of social problems. The means to the end can only originate in material reality.

The new spiritual life has been passed on by the leading classes to the proletarian intellect in a devitalized form. It is of primary importance that this be understood when considering the forces to be utilized in solving the social question. Should this state of affairs remain unchanged, the spiritual life of mankind will be condemned to impotence as far as the social challenges of the present and the future are concerned. A majority of the modern proletariat is absolutely convinced of this impotence, a belief which is brought to expression through Marxism and similar confessions. It is said that modern capitalism has evolved from older economic forms, that this evolution has placed the proletariat in an untenable position with respect to capital, that the evolution will continue until capitalism destroys itself by means of the forces inherent in it and that the liberation of the proletariat will coincide with the death of capitalism. Later socialist thinkers have divested this conviction of the fatalistic character assigned to it by certain Marxist circles. Nevertheless, its essential nature remains, as is evidenced by the fact that it would not occur to a contemporary socialist to say that the incentive for the social movement could derive from an interior life born of impulses of the times and which has its roots in spiritual reality.

The mental attitude of the person forced to lead a proletarian life is determined by the fact that he cannot cherish such expectations. He needs a spiritual life which emanates the strength to enable him to sense his human dignity. Being harnessed to the modern capitalistic economic order, his soul necessarily thirsted for some such spiritual life. But the spiritual life handed to him by the ruling classes created an emptiness in his soul. The present-day social movement is determined by the fact that the modern proletarian desires a quite different relationship to spiritual life than the contemporary social order can give him; and this is what is behind his demands. This fact is clearly understood neither by the proletariat nor by the non-proletarian. The non-proletarian does not suffer under the ideological label (of his own making) attached to spiritual life. The proletarian does. And this ideological label has robbed him of belief in the sustaining value of spiritual values as such. Finding the way out of the present chaotic social situation depends upon a correct insight into this fact. Access to this way has been closed by the social order which has evolved, along with the new economic forms, under the influence of the ruling classes. The strength to open it must be acquired.

There will be a complete change of attitude concerning this subject when sufficient importance has been attributed to the fact that a society of men and women in which spiritual life functions as an ideology lacks one of the forces which makes the social organism viable. Contemporary society has become ill due to the impotence of spiritual life, and the illness is aggravated by reluctance to recognize its existence. By recognizing this fact we would acquire the foundation on which ideas could be developed which are truly appropriate to the social movement.

The proletarian believes that he touches on one of his soul's basic strengths when he talks of class consciousness. The truth, however, is that ever since he has been harnessed to the capitalistic economic order, he has been seeking a spiritual life, one which can sustain his soul and make him conscious of his dignity as a human being. But a spiritual life considered to be ideology is not able to develop this consciousness. He has sought this consciousness, and when he could not find it, he substituted the concept of class consciousness.

His gaze is directed exclusively toward economic factors, as though drawn there by a powerfully suggestive force. He therefore no longer believes that the impetus necessary to accomplish something positive in the social field can be found anywhere else. He believes that only the evolution of the spiritless, soulless economic life can bring about conditions which he feels correspond to human dignity. He is therefore forced to seek his salvation in the transformation of economic life. He is forced to conclude that through the transformation of economic life all the injuries will disappear which derive from private enterprise, from the individual employer's egotism and inability to satisfy the employees' demands for human dignity. Thus, the modern proletariat has come to see the only remedy for the social organism in the transfer of all privately owned means of production to community operation or even community [state] property. This opinion was possible because we have diverted our attention from spiritual forces and concentrated solely on the economic process.

This is the source of the contradictory elements in the proletariat movement. The modern proletarian believes that he will attain to his rights as a human being through developments in the economic field. He is fighting for these rights. And yet, in the process something appears which could never be the result of economic activities alone. This phenomenon, which is thought to be the consequence of economic factors alone, is a very salient feature of the social question. It is a process which follows a direct line of development from ancient slavery through the serfdom of the middle ages and up to the modern proletariat. The circulation of commodities and money, the realities of capital, real estate, private property and so forth, are all elements of modern life. A characteristic of contemporary society which is not clearly identified, not even consciously recognized by the proletarian but which constitutes the fundamental impulse for his social will, is that the modern capitalistic economic order, within its own sphere of activity, recognizes only commodities and their respective values. Within this capitalistic organism something has become a commodity which the proletarian feels cannot be a commodity.

The modern proletarian abhors instinctively, unconsciously, the fact that he must sell his labor power to his employer in the same way that commodities are sold in the market, and that the law of supply and demand plays its role in determining the value of his labor just as it does in determining the value of commodities. This abhorrence of the commodity nature of work has a profound meaning in the social movement. Not even the socialist theories emphasize this point radically enough. This is the second element which makes the social question so urgent; the first being the conviction that spiritual life is an ideology.

In antiquity there were slaves. The whole person was sold like a commodity. Somewhat less of him, but a substantial part of the human being nonetheless, was incorporated into the economic process by serfdom. Capitalism is the force which persists in giving a commodity nature to a portion of the human being: his labor power. I do not mean to imply that this has not been recognized. On the contrary, it is recognized as a fact of fundamental importance in the modern social movement. Nevertheless, it is considered to be of an economic nature, and the question of the commodity nature of labor is therewith turned solely into a question of economics. It is erroneously believed that solutions will be found in economic factors through which the proletarian will cease to consider the incorporation of his labor power in society as unworthy of human dignity. How modern economic forms evolved historically and how they gave human labor power a commodity character is understood. What is not understood is that it is inherent in economic life that everything incorporated into it must take on the nature of a commodity. It is not possible to divest human labor of its commodity character without first finding a means of extracting it from the economic process. Efforts should therefore not be directed towards transforming the economic process so that human labor power is justly treated within it, but towards extracting labor power from the economic process and integrating it with social forces which will relieve it of its commodity character. The proletarian yearns for an economic life in which his labor can assume its rightful place. He does so because he does not see that the commodity character of his labor is the result of his being totally harnessed to the economic process. Due to the fact that he must deliver up his labor to the economic process, he necessarily delivers up himself along with it. The economic process, by its very nature, tends to utilize labor in the most expedient manner and will continue to do so as long as labor regulation remains one of its functions. As though hypnotized by the power of modern economics, all eyes are focused on what it alone can accomplish. However, the means through which labor power no longer need be a commodity will not be found in this direction. A different economic form will only convert labor into a commodity in a different way. The labor question cannot be properly integrated into the social question until it is recognized that the production, distribution and consumption of commodities are determined by interests which should not extend to human labor power.

The thinking of our times has not learned to differentiate between two essentially different functions in economic life: on the one hand labor, which is intimately associated with the human being, and on the other hand the production-distribution-consumption process, which essentially is not. Should sound thinking along these lines make manifest the true nature of the labor question, then this same type of thinking will indicate the position economic life is to assume in a healthy social organism.

It is already apparent that the 'social question' may be conceived of as three particular questions. The first pertains to the healthy form spiritual-cultural life should assume in the social organism; the second deals with the just integration of labor in the community, and the third concerns the way the economy should function within this community.

Chapter Two

Finding Real Solutions to the Social Problems of the Times

The characteristic element which has given the social question its particular form in modern times may be described as follows. The economy, along with technology and modern capitalism, has, as a matter of course, brought a certain inner order to modern society. While the attention of humanity has focused on what technology and capitalism have brought, it has been diverted from other branches, other areas of the social organism. It is equally necessary to attain efficacy through human consciousness in these areas if the social organism is to become healthy.

In order to clearly characterize certain driving forces by means of a comprehensive, universal observation of the social organism, I would like to start with a comparison. It should be borne in mind, however, that nothing more than a comparison is intended. Human understanding can be assisted by such a comparison to form mental pictures about the social organism's restoration to health. To consider the most complicated of all-natural organisms, the human organism, from the point of view presented here, it is necessary to direct our attention to the fact that the total essence of this human organism exhibits three complementary systems, each of which functions with a certain autonomy. These three complementary systems can be characterized as follows. The system consisting of the nerve and sense faculties functions as one area in the natural human organism. It could also be designated, after the most important member of the organism in which the nerve and sense faculties are to a certain extent centralized, the head-organism.

A clear understanding of the human organization will result in recognizing as the second member what I would like to call the rhythmic system. It consists of respiration, blood circulation and everything which expresses itself in the rhythmic processes of the human organism.

The third system is to be recognized in everything which, in the form of organs and functions, is connected with metabolism as such. These three systems contain everything which, when properly coordinated, maintains the entire functioning of the human organism in a healthy manner.*

[* The arrangement meant here is not a spatial delimitation of the bodily members, but is according to the activities (functions) of the organism. The term 'head-organism' is only to be used in that one is aware that the nerve-sense faculty is principally centralized in the head. Of course the rhythmic and metabolic functions are also present in the head, as is the nerve-sense faculty in the other bodily members. Nevertheless, the three functional types are, according to their natures, separated.]

In my book "Von Seelenrätseln"[4] I have attempted to characterize, at least in outline, this triformation of the human natural organism. It is clear to me that biology, physiology, natural science as a whole will, in the very near future, tend toward a consideration of the human organism which perceives how these three members – the head-system, the circulatory system or breast-system and the metabolic system maintain the processes in the human organism, how they function with a certain autonomy, how no absolute centralization of the human organism exists and how each of these systems has its own particular relation to the outer world. The head-system through the senses, the circulatory or rhythmic system through respiration and the metabolic system through the organs of nourishment and movement.

---

[4] *Von Seelenräteln.* Extracts from this book have been published by the Rudolf Steiner Press, London. 1970, under the title *The Case for Anthroposophy*, selected, translated, arranged and with an introduction by Owen Barfield.

Natural scientific methods are not yet sufficiently advanced for scientific circles to be able to grant recognition, sufficient for an advance in knowledge, to what I have indicated here, which is an attempt to utilize knowledge based on spiritual science for natural scientific purposes.

This means, however, that our way of thinking, the whole way in which we conceive of the world, is not yet completely in accordance with how, for example, the inner essence of nature's functions manifests itself in the human organism. One could very well say: yes, but natural science can wait, its ideals will develop gradually, and it will come to a point where viewpoints such as these will be recognized. It is not possible, however, to wait where these things are concerned. In every human soul — for every human mind takes part in the functioning of the social organism — and not only in the minds of a few specialists, at least an instinctive knowledge of what this social organism needs, must be present. Healthy thinking and feeling, healthy will and aspirations with regard to the organization of the social organism, can only develop when it is clear, albeit more or less instinctively, that in order for the social organism to be healthy it must, like the natural organism, have a threefold organization.

Ever since Schäffle wrote his book about the structure of the social organism, attempts have been made to encounter analogies between the organization of a natural being, the human being for example, and human society as such. The cell of the social organism has been sought, the cell structure, tissues and so forth! A short while ago a book by Meray appeared, Weltmutation (World Mutation), in which certain scientific facts and laws were simply transferred to a supposed human society-organism. What is meant here has absolutely nothing to do with all these analogy games. To assume that in my considerations such an analogy game between the natural and the social organism is being played is to reveal a failure to enter into the spirit of what is here meant. No attempt is being made to transplant some scientific fact to the social organism; quite the contrary. It is rather intended that human thinking and feeling learn to sense the vital potentialities in contemplating the natural organism and then to be capable of applying this sensibility to the social organism. When what has supposedly been learned about the natural organism is simply transferred to the social organism, this only indicates an unwillingness to acquire the capacity to contemplate and investigate the social organism just as independently as is necessary for an understanding of the natural organism. If, in order to perceive its laws, one considers the social organism as an independent entity in the same manner as a scientific investigator considers the natural organism, in that instant the seriousness of the contemplation excludes playing with analogies.

It may also be imagined that what is presented here is based on the belief that the social organism should be constructed as an imitation of some bleak scientific theory. Nothing could be farther from the truth. It is my intention to point out something quite different. The present historical human crisis requires that certain sensibilities arise in every individual, that these sensibilities be stimulated by education, i.e., the school system, as is the learning of arithmetical functions. What has hitherto resulted from the old forms of the social organism, without being consciously absorbed by the inner life of the soul, will cease be effective in the future. A characteristic of the evolutionary impulses which are attempting to manifest themselves in human life at the present time is that such sensibilities are necessary, just as schooling has long been a necessity. From now on mankind should acquire a healthy sense of how the social organism should function in order for it to be viable. A feeling must be acquired that it is unhealthy and anti-social to want to participate in this organism without such sensibilities.

It is often said that 'socialization' is needed for these times. This socialization will not be a curative process for the social organism, but a quack remedy, perhaps even a destructive process, as long as at least an instinctive knowledge of the necessity for the tri-formation of the social organism has not been absorbed by human hearts, by human minds. If this social organism is to function in a healthy way it must methodically cultivate three constituent members.

One of these members is the economy. It will be considered first because it has so evidently been able to dominate human society through modern technology and capitalism. This economic must constitute an autonomous member within the social organism, as relatively autonomous as is the nervous-sensory system in the human organism. The economy is concerned with all aspects of the production, circulation and consumption of commodities.

The second member of the social organism is that of civil rights, of political life as such. What can be designated as the state, in the sense of the old rights-state, pertains to this member. Whereas the economy is concerned with all aspects of man's natural needs and the production, circulation and consumption of commodities, this second member of the social organism can only concern itself with all aspects of the relations between human beings which derive from purely human sources. It is essential for knowledge about the members of the social organism to be able to differentiate between the legal rights system, which can only concern itself with relations between human beings that derive from human sources, and the economic system, which can only be concerned with the production, circulation and consumption of commodities. It is necessary to sense this difference in order that, as a consequence of this sensibility, the economy be separate from the political rights member, as in the human natural organism the activity of the lungs in processing the outside air is separate from the processes of the nervous-sensory system.

The third member, standing autonomous alongside the other two, is to be apprehended in the social organism as that which pertains to spiritual life. To be more precise, because the designations 'spiritual culture' or 'everything which pertains to spiritual life,' are perhaps not sufficiently precise, one could say: everything which is based on the natural aptitudes of each human individual; what must enter into the social organism based on the natural aptitudes, spiritual as well as physical, of each individual. The first sphere, the economic, is concerned with what must be present in order for man to determine his relation to the outer world. The second sphere is concerned with what must be present in the social organism in respect to human inter-relationships. The third sphere is concerned with everything which must blossom forth from each human individuality and be integrated into the social organism.

Just as it is true that modern technology and capitalism have molded our society in recent times, it is also imperative that the wounds necessarily inflicted on human society by them be thoroughly healed by correctly relating man and the human community to the three members of the social organism. The economy has, of itself, taken on quite definite forms in recent times. Through one-sided efficiency, it has exerted an especially powerful influence on human life. Until now the other two members of society have not been in a position to properly integrate themselves in the social organism with the same certitude and according to their own laws. It is therefore necessary that each individual, in the place where he or she happens to be, undertakes to work for social formation based on the sensibilities described above. It is inherent in these attempts at solving the social questions that in the present and in the immediate future each individual has his social task.

The first member of the social organism, the economy, depends primarily on nature, just as the individual, in respect to what he can make of himself through education and experience, depends on the aptitudes of his spiritual and physical organisms. This natural base simply impresses itself on the economy, and thereby on the entire social organism. It is there and cannot be affected essentially by any social organization, by any socialization. It must constitute the foundation of the social organism, as the human being's aptitudes in various areas, his natural physical and spiritual abilities, must constitute the foundation of his education. Every attempt at socialization, at giving human society an economic structure, must take the natural base into account. This elementary, primitive element which binds the human being to a certain piece of nature, constitutes the foundation for the circulation of goods, all human labor and every form of cultural-spiritual life. It is necessary to take the relationship of the social organism to its natural base into consideration, just as it is necessary to take the relationship of the individual to his aptitudes into consideration where the learning process is concerned. This can be made clear by citing extreme cases. In certain regions of the earth, where the banana is an easily accessible food, what is taken into consideration is the labor which must be expended in order to transfer the bananas from their place of origin to a certain destination and convert them into items of consumption. If the human labor which must be expended in order to make the bananas consumer items for society is compared with the labor which must be expended in Central Europe to do the same with wheat, it will be seen that the labor necessary for the bananas is at least three hundred times less than for the wheat. Of course, that is an extreme case. Nevertheless, such differences in the required amount of labor in relation to the natural base are also present in the branches of production which are represented in any European society, not as radically as with the bananas and wheat, but the differences do exist. It is thereby substantiated that the amount of labor power which men must bring to the economic process is conditioned by the natural base of their economy. In Germany, for example, in regions of average fertility, the wheat yield is approximately seven to eight times the amount sown; in Chile the yield is twelve-fold, in northern Mexico seventeen-fold, and in Peru twenty-fold.[5]

The entire homogeneous entity consisting of processes which begin with man's relation to nature and continue through his activities in transforming the products of nature into consumable goods, all these processes, and only these, comprise the economic member of a healthy social organism. This member is comparable to the head system of the human organism which conditions individual aptitudes and, just as this head-system is dependent on the lung-heart system, the economic system is dependent on human labor. But the head cannot independently regulate breathing; nor should the human labor system be regulated by the same forces which control the economy.

The human being is engaged in economic activity in his own interests. These are based on his spiritual needs and on the needs of his soul. How these interests can be most suitably approached within a social organism so

---

[5] Carl Jentsch Volkswirtschaftslehre (Economics) published 1895.

that the individual can best satisfy his interests through the social organism and also be economically active to the best advantage, is a question which must be resolved in practice within the various economic facilities. This can only happen if the interests are able to freely assert themselves, and if the will and possibility arise to do what is necessary to satisfy them. The origin of the interests lies beyond the circle which circumscribes economic affairs. They develop together with the development of the human soul and body. The task of economic life is to establish facilities in order to satisfy them. These facilities should be exclusively concerned with the production and interchange of commodities, that is, of goods which acquire value through human need. The commodity has value through the person who consumes it. Due to the fact that the commodity acquires its value through the consumer, its position in the social organism is completely different from the other things which the human being, as a member of this organism, values. The economy, within the circumference of which the production, inter-change and consumption of commodities belong, should be considered without preconceptions. The essential difference between the person-to-person relationship in which one produces commodities for the other, and the rights relationship as such will be evident. Careful consideration will lead to the conviction and the practical requirement that in the social organism legal rights must be completely separated from the economic sector. The activities which are to be carried out in the facilities which serve the production and interchange of commodities are not conducive to the best possible influence on the area of human rights. In the economy one individual turns to another individual because one serves the interests of the other, but the relation of one person to another is fundamentally different in the area of human rights.

It might seem that the required distinction would be sufficiently realized if the legal rights element, which must also exist in the relations between the persons engaged in the economy, be provided for in it. Such a belief has no foundation in reality. The individual can only correctly experience the rights relation, which must exist between himself and others, when he does not experience this relation in the economic area, but in an area which is separate from it. Therefore, an area must develop in the social organism alongside the economy and independent of it, in which the rights element is cultivated and administered. The rights element is, moreover, that of the political domain, of the state. If people carry over their economic interests into the legislation and administration of the rights-state, then the resulting rights will only be the expression of these economic interests. When the rights-state manages the economy, it loses the ability to guarantee human rights. Its acts and facilities will serve the need for commodities;

they are therefore diverted from the actions which correspond to human rights.

The healthy social organism requires an autonomous political state as the second member alongside the economic sector. In the autonomous economic sector, through the forces of economic life, people will develop facilities which will best serve the production and interchange of commodities. In the political state facilities will develop which will orient the mutual relations between persons and groups in a way which corresponds to human rights-awareness.

This viewpoint, which advocates the complete separation of rights-state and economy, is one which corresponds to the realities of life. The same cannot be said for the viewpoint which would merge the economic and rights functions. Those who are active in the economic sector do, of course, possess a rights-awareness; but their participation in legislative and administrative processes will derive exclusively from this rights-awareness only if their judgment in this area occurs within the framework of a rights-state which does not occupy itself with economic matters. Such a rights-state has its own legislative and administrative bodies, both structured according to the principles which derive from the modern rights awareness. It will be structured according to the impulses in human consciousness nowadays referred to as democratic. The economic area will form its legislative and administrative bodies in accordance with economic impulses. The necessary contact between the responsible persons of the rights and economic bodies will ensue in a manner similar to that at present practiced by the governments of different sovereign states. Through this formation the developments in one body will be able to have the necessary effect on developments in the other. As things are now this effect is hindered by one area trying to develop in itself what should flow toward it from the other.

The economy is subject, on the one hand, to the conditions of the natural base (climate, regional geography, mineral wealth and so forth) and, on the other hand, it is dependent upon the legal conditions which the state imposes between the persons or groups engaged in economic activity. The boundaries of what economic activity can and should encompass are therefore laid out. Just as nature imposes prerequisites from the outside on the economic process which those engaged in economic activity take for granted as something upon which they must build this economy, so should everything which underlies the legal relationship between persons be regulated, in a healthy social organism, by a rights-state which, like the natural base, is autonomous in its relation to the economy.

In the social organism that has evolved through history and which, by means of the machine age and modern capitalism has given the social movement its characteristic stamp, economic activity encompasses more than is good for a healthy social organism. In today's economic sphere, in which only commodities should circulate, human labor and rights circulate as well. In the economic process of today, which is based on the division of labor, not only are commodities exchanged for commodities, but commodities are exchanged for both labor and for rights. (I call commodity everything which has been prepared by human activity for consumption and brought to a certain locality for this purpose. Although this description may be objectionable or seem insufficient to some economists, it can nevertheless be useful for an understanding of just what should belong to economic activity.) When someone acquires a piece of land through purchase, the process must be considered an exchange of the land for commodities, represented by the purchase money. The land itself, however, does not act as a commodity in economic life. Its position is based on the right of a person to use it. This right is essentially different from the relationship in which the producer of a commodity finds himself. This relationship, by its very nature, does not overlap with the completely different type of person-to-person relationship which results from the fact that someone has the exclusive use of a piece of land. The owner puts those persons who earn their living on the land as his employees, or those who must live on it, in a position of dependence on him. The exchange of real commodities which are produced or consumed does not cause a dependence which has the same effect as this personal kind of relationship.

Looking at this fact of life impartially, one sees clearly that it must find expression in the institutions of the entire social organism. As long as commodities are exchanged for other commodities in the economic sphere, the value of these commodities is determined independently of the legal relations between persons or groups. As soon as commodities are exchanged for rights, however, the legal relations themselves are affected. It is not a question of the exchange itself. This is a necessary, vital element of the contemporary social organism based on its division of labor; the problem is that through the exchange of rights for commodities the rights become commodities when they originate within the economic sphere. This can only be avoided by the existence of facilities in the social organism which, on the one hand, have the exclusive function of activating the circulation of commodities in the most expedient manner, and, on the other hand, facilities which regulate the rights, inherent in the commodity exchange process, of those individuals who produce, trade and consume. These rights are essentially no different from other rights of a personal nature which exist independently of the commodity exchange process. If I injure or benefit my fellow-man through the sale of a commodity, this belongs in the same social category as an injury or benefit through an act or omission not directly related to commodity exchange.

The individual's life is influenced by rights institutions [states] acting together with economic interests. In a healthy social organism these influences must come from two different directions. In the economic organization formal training, together with experience, is to provide management with the necessary insights. Through law and administration in the rights organization the necessary rights-awareness, in respect to the relations of individuals, or groups of individuals, to each other will be realized. The economic organization will allow persons with similar professional or consumer interests, or with similar needs of other kinds, to unite in cooperative associations which, will organize the economy. This organization will structure itself on an associative foundation and on the interrelations between associations. The associations will engage in purely economic activities. The legal basis for their work will be provided by the rights-state. When such economic associations are able to make their economic interests felt in the representative and administrative bodies of the economic organization, they will not feel the need to pressure the legislative or administrative leadership of the rights-state (for example, farmers' and industrialists' lobbies, economically orientated social democrats) in order to attain there what is not attainable within the economic sector. If the rights state is not active in any economic field, then it will only establish facilities which derive from the rights awareness of the persons involved. Even if the same individuals who are active in the economic area also participate in the representation of the rights-state, which would of course be the case, no economic influence can be exerted on the rights sector, due to the formation of separate economic and rights systems. Such influence undermines the health of the social organism, as it can also be undermined when the state itself manages branches of the economic sector and when representatives of economic interests determine laws in accordance with those interests.

Austria offered a typical example of the fusion of the economic and rights sectors with the constitution it adopted in the eighteen-sixties. The representatives of the imperial assembly of this territorial union were elected from the ranks of the four economic branches: The land owners, the chamber of commerce, the cities, markets and industrial areas, and the rural communities. It is clear from this composition of the representative assembly that they thought a rights system would ensue by allowing economic interests to exert themselves. Certainly the divergent forces of its many nationalities contributed a great deal to Austria's disintegration. It is equally certain, however, that a rights organization functioning alongside the economy would have enabled the development of a form of society in which the co-existence of the various nationalities would have been possible.

Nowadays people interested in public life usually direct their attention to matters of secondary importance. They do this because their thinking habits induce them to consider the social organism as a uniform entity. A suitable elective process for such an entity is not to be found. Regardless of the elective process employed, economic interests and the impulses emanating from the rights sector will conflict with each other in the representative bodies. This conflict must result in extreme social agitation. Priority must be given today to the all-important objective of working toward a drastic separation of the economy from the rights-organization. As this separation becomes a reality, the separating organizations will, each according to their own principles, find the best means of choosing their legislators and administrators. This question of how to choose such representatives, although as such of fundamental significance, is secondary compared to the other pressing decisions which must be made today. Where old conditions still exist, these new forms could be developed from them. Where the old has already disintegrated, or is in the process of doing so, individuals or groups of individuals should take the initiative in attempting to reorganize society in the indicated direction. To expect an overnight transformation is seen even by reasonable socialists as unrealistic. They expect the healing process which they desire to be gradual and relevant. However, that the historical human evolutionary forces of today make a rational desire for a new social structure necessary is perfectly obvious to every objective person who observes current events.

One who considers practical only what he has become accustomed to within the limits of his own horizons, will consider what is presented here as impractical. If he is not able to change his attitude however, and has influence in some area, his actions will not contribute to the healing, but to the continued degeneration of the social organism, just as the deeds of people of like mind have contributed to present conditions.

The endeavors which have already begun to be realized by those in authority to turn certain economic functions over to the state must be reversed; the state must be relieved of all economic functions. Thinkers who like to believe that they are on the road to a healthy social organism carry these efforts at nationalization to their logically extreme conclusions. They desire the socialization of all economic means, insofar as they are means of production. Healthy development, however, requires that the economy be autonomous, and the political state be able, through the process of law, to affect economic organizations in such a way that the individual does not feel that his integration in the social organism is in conflict with his rights-awareness.

It is possible to see how the ideas presented here are based on the realities of the human situation by directing one's attention to the physical labor which the human being performs for the social organism. Within the capitalistic economy, this labor has been incorporated into the social organism in such a way that it is bought like a commodity from the worker by his employer. An exchange takes place between money (representing commodities) and labor. But such an exchange cannot, in reality, take place. It only appears to do so.* In reality, the employer receives commodities from the worker, which can only come into existence by the worker devoting his labor-power to their creation. The worker receives one part of the equivalent value of these commodities and the employer the other. The production of commodities results from the cooperation of the employer and the employed. Only the product of their joint action passes into economic circulation. A legal relationship between worker and entrepreneur is necessary for the production of the commodity. Capitalism, however, converts this relationship into one which is determined by the economic supremacy of the employer over the worker. In the healthy social organism, it will be apparent that labor cannot be paid for. It cannot attain an economic value through equivalence with a commodity. These, produced by labor, acquire value through equivalence with other commodities. The kind and amount of work, as well as the way in which the individual performs it for the maintenance of the social organism, must be determined by his own abilities as well as the requisites for a decent human existence. This is only possible if the determination is carried out by the political state independent of economic interests.

Through this determination the commodity will acquire a value basis which is comparable to that which exists in the conditions imposed by nature. As the value of a commodity increases in relation to another commodity due to the acquisition of the raw materials necessary for its production becoming more difficult, so must its value also be dependent upon the kind and amount of labor which may be expended for its production in accordance with rights legislation.** In this way the economy becomes subject to two essential conditions: that of the natural base, which humanity must take as it is given, and that of the rights base, which should be created through a rights-awareness with roots in a political state independent of economic interests.

It is evident that by organizing the social organism in this way, economic prosperity will increase and decrease according to the amount of labor rights-awareness decides to expend. In a healthy social organism it is necessary that economic prosperity be dependent in this way, for only such dependence can prevent man from being so consumed by economic interests that he can no longer consider his existence worthy of human dignity. And, in truth, all the turmoil in the social organism results from the feeling that existence is unworthy of human dignity.

[* It is not only possible for processes in life to be explained falsely, they can also occur falsely. Money and labor are not inter-changeable values as are money and the products of labor Therefore, if I give money for labor, I do something false. I create a deception. In reality, I can only give money for the products of labor.]

[** Such a relationship of labor to rights legislation will compel the economic associations to accept what is 'just' as a precondition. Thereby a condition will be attained in which the economic organization is dependent on people, and not vice-verse.]

A comparison with the means employed to improve the natural base can be used to find possible means of avoiding steep declines in prosperity as an effect of the rights sector's measures.

A low yield soil can be made more productive through the use of technical means; similarly, if prosperity declines excessively the type and amount of labor can be modified. This modification should not emanate directly from economic circles, but from the insight which can develop in a rights organization which is independent of economic life.

Everything which occurs in the social organization due to economic activity and rights-awareness is influenced by what emanates from a third source: the individual abilities of each human being. This includes the greatest spiritual accomplishments as well as superior or inferior physical aptitudes. What derives from this source must be introduced into the healthy social organism in quite a different manner than the exchange of commodities or what emanates from the state. This introduction can only be effected in a sound manner if it is left to man's free receptivity and the impulses which come from individual abilities. The human efforts and achievements which result from such abilities are, to a great extent, deprived of the true essence of their being if they are influenced by economic interests or the political state. This essence can only exist in the forces which human effort and achievement must develop of and by themselves. Free receptivity, the only suitable means, is paralyzed when the social integration of these efforts and achievements is directly conditioned by economic interests or organized by the state. There is only one possible healthy form of development for spiritual-cultural life: what it produces shall be the result of its own impulses and a relationship of mutual understanding shall exist between itself and the recipients of its achievements. (The development of the individual abilities present in society is connected to the development of spiritual life by countless fine threads.)

The conditions described here for the healthy development of spiritual-cultural life are not recognized today because powers of observation have been clouded by the fusion of a large part of this life with the political state. This fusion has come about in the course of the past centuries and we have grown accustomed to it. There is talk, of course, of 'scientific and educational freedom.' It is taken for granted however, that the political state should administer the 'free science' and the 'free education.' It is not understood that in this way the state makes spiritual life dependent on state requirements. People think that the state can provide the educational facilities and that the teachers who occupy them can develop culture and spiritual life 'freely' in them. This opinion ignores how closely related the content of spiritual life is to the innermost essence of the human being in which it is developing, and how this development can only be free when it is introduced into the social organism through the impulses which originate in spiritual life itself, and through no others. Through fusion with the state, not only the administration of science and the part of spiritual life connected with it has been determined, but the content as well. Of course what mathematics or physics produce cannot be directly influenced by the state. But the history of the cultural and social sciences shows that they have become reflections of their representatives' relations to the state and of state requirements. Due to this phenomenon, the contemporary scientifically oriented concepts which dominate spiritual life affect the proletarian as ideology. He has noticed how certain aspects of human thought are determined by state requirements which correspond to the interests of the ruling classes. The proletarian saw therein a reflection of material interests as well as a battle of conflicting interests. This created the feeling that all spiritual life is ideology, a reflection of economic organization.

This desolating view of human spiritual life ceases when the feeling can arise that in the spiritual sphere a self-containing reality, transcending the material element, is at work. It is impossible for such a feeling to arise when spiritual life is not freely self-developing and administered within the social organism. Only those persons who are active in the development and administration of spiritual-cultural life have the strength to secure its appropriate place in the social organism. Art, science, philosophical world-views, and all that goes with them, need just such an independent position in human society, for in spiritual life everything is interrelated. The freedom of one cannot flourish without the freedom of the other. Although the content of mathematics and physics cannot be directly influenced by state requirements, what develops from them, what people think of their value, what effects their cultivation can have on the rest of spiritual-cultural life, and much more, is conditioned by these requirements when the state administers branches of spiritual life. It is very different if a teacher of the lowest school grades follows the impulses of the state or if she receives these impulses from a spiritual life which is self-contained. The Social Democrats have merely inherited the habits of thought and the customs of the ruling classes in this respect. Their ideal is to include spiritual-cultural life in social institutions which are organized upon economic principles. If they succeed in reaching their goal, they will only have continued along the path of spiritual depreciation. They were correct, although one-sided, in their demand that religion be a private affair. In a healthy social organism, all spiritual life must be, in respect to the state and the economy, a 'private affair.' But the social democrats' motive in wanting to transfer religion to the private sector is not a desire to create a position within the social organism where a spiritual institution would develop in a more desirable, worthier manner than it can under state influence. They are of the opinion that the social organism should only cultivate with its own means its own necessities of life. And religious values do not belong to this category. A branch of spiritual life cannot flourish when it is unilaterally removed from the public sector in this way, if the other spiritual branches remain fettered. Modern humanity's religious life will only develop its soul-sustaining strength together with all the other liberated branches of spiritual life.

Not only the creation but also the reception by humanity of this spiritual life must be freely determined in accordance with the soul's necessities. Teachers, artists and such whose only direct connection with a state legislature or administration is with those which have their origin in spiritual life itself, will be able, through their actions, to inspire the development of a receptivity for their efforts and achievements among individuals who are protected by a self-reliant, independent political state from being forced to exist only for work, and which guarantees their right to a leisure that can awaken in them an appreciation of spiritual values. Those persons who imagine themselves to be practical may object that people would pass their leisure time drinking and that illiteracy would result if the state occupied itself with the right to leisure and if school attendance were left to free human common sense. Let these pessimists wait and see what will happen when the world is no longer under their influence, all too often determined by a certain feeling which, whispering in their ear, reminds them of how they use their leisure time, what they needed to acquire a little learning. They cannot imagine the power of enthusiasm which a really self-contained spiritual life can have in the social organism, because the fettered one they know cannot exert such an enthusiastic influence over them.

Both the political state and the economy will receive the spiritual performance they require from a self-administered spiritual-cultural organism. Furthermore, practical economic training will reach full effectiveness through free cooperation with this organism. People who have received the appropriate training will be able to vitalize their economic experience through the strength that will come to them from liberated spiritual values. Those with economic experience will also work for the spiritual-cultural organization, where their abilities are most needed.

In the political area, the necessary insights will be formed through the activation of spiritual values. The worker will acquire, through the influence of such spiritual values, a feeling of satisfaction in respect to the function his labor performs in the social organism. He will realize that without management organizing labor in a meaningful way the social organism could not support him. He will sense the need for cooperation between his work and the organizing abilities which derive from the development of individual human abilities. Within the framework of the political state he will acquire the rights which insure his share of the commodities he produces; and he will freely grant an appropriate share of the proceeds for the formation of the spiritual values which flow toward him. In the field of spiritual-cultural life, it will become possible for those engaged in creative activities to live from the proceeds of their efforts. What someone practices in the field of spiritual life is his own affair. What he is able to contribute to the social organism however, will be recompensed by those who have need of his spiritual contribution. Whoever is not able to support himself within the spiritual organization from such compensation will have to transfer his activities to the political or economic sphere of activity.

The technical ideas that derive from spiritual life flow into the economic sector. They derive from spiritual life even when they come directly from members of the state or economic sectors. All organizational ideas and forces which fecundate the economic and state sectors originate in spiritual life. Compensation for this input to both social sectors will come either through the free appreciation of the beneficiaries, or through laws determined by the political state. Tax laws will provide this political state with what it needs to maintain itself. These will be devised through a harmonization of 'rights awareness' and economic requirements.

In a healthy social organism the autonomous spiritual sector must function alongside the political and economic sectors. The evolutionary forces in modern mankind point toward a threefold formation of this organism. As long as society was essentially governed by instinctive forces, the urge for this formation did not arise. What actually derived from three sources functioned somewhat torpidly together in society. Modern times demand the individual's conscious participation in this organism. This consciousness can only give the individual's behavior and whole life a healthy form if it is oriented from three sources. Modern man, in the unconscious depths of his soul, strives toward this orientation; and what manifests itself in the social movement is only the dim reflection of this striving.

Toward the end of the eighteenth century, under different circumstances than those under which we live at present, a call for a new formation of the human social organism arose from the depths of human nature. The motto of this reorganization consisted of three words: fraternity, equality, liberty. Anyone with an objective mind who considers the realities of human social development with healthy sensibilities, cannot help but be sympathetic to the meaning behind these words. However, during the course of the nineteenth century, some very clever thinkers took pains to point out the impossibility of realizing these ideals of fraternity, equality and liberty in a uniform social organism. They felt certain that these three impulses would be contradictory if practiced in society. It was clearly demonstrated, for example, that individual freedom would not be possible if the equality principle were practiced One is obliged to agree with those who observed these contradictions; nevertheless, one must at the same time feel sympathy for each of these ideals.

These contradictions exist because the true social meaning of these three ideals only becomes evident through an understanding of the necessary threefold formation of the social organism. The three members are not to be united and centralized in some abstract, theoretical parliamentary body. Each of the three members is to be centralized within itself, and then, through their mutual cooperation, the unity of the overall social organism can come about. In real life, the apparent contradictions act as a unifying element. An apprehension of the living social organism can be attained when one is able to observe the true formation of this organism with respect to fraternity, equality and liberty. It will then be evident that human cooperation in economic life must be based on the fraternity which is inherent in associations. In the second member, the civil rights state, which is concerned with purely human, person-to-person relations, it is necessary to strive for the realization of the idea of equality. And in the relatively independent spiritual sector of the social organism it is necessary to strive for the realization of the idea of freedom. Seen in this light, the real worth of these three ideals becomes clear. They cannot be realized in a chaotic society, but only in a healthy, threefold social organism. No abstract, centralized social structure is able to realize the ideals of liberty, equality and fraternity in such disarrangement; but each of the three sectors of the social organism can draw strength from one of these impulses and cooperate in a positive manner with the other sectors.

Those individuals who demanded and worked for the realization of the three ideas — liberty, equality and fraternity — as well as those who later followed in their footsteps, were able to dimly discern in which direction modern humanity's forces of evolution are pointing. But they have not been able to overcome their belief in the uniform state, so their ideas contain a contradictory element. Nevertheless, they remained faithful to the contradictory, for in the subconscious depths of their souls the impulse toward the threefold formation of the social organism, in which their ideals can attain to a higher unity, continued to exert itself. The clearly discernible social facts of contemporary life demand that the forces of evolution, which in modern mankind strive toward this threefold formation, be turned into conscious will.

Chapter Three

Capitalism and Social Ideas (Capital, Human Labor)

I t is not possible to judge what kind of action is demanded by the events of the times without the will to be guided in this judgment by an insight into the basic forces of the social organism. The preceding presentation is an attempt to arrive at such an insight. Measures based on a judgment which derives from a narrowly circumscribed field of observation cannot have positive results today. The facts which have grown out of the social movement reveal disturbances in the foundations of the social organism, and by no means superficial ones. Therefore, it is necessary to arrive at insights which penetrate to these foundations.

When capital and capitalism are spoken of today, they refer to what proletarian humanity considers to be the causes of its oppression. It is only possible to form a worthwhile judgment concerning the way in which capital furthers or hinders the social organism's circulatory processes by perceiving how individual human capabilities, rights legislation and the forces of economic life produce and consume capital. When human labor is spoken of it refers to the function that, together with the natural base of the economy and capital, creates the economic values through which the worker becomes conscious of his social condition. A judgment as to how this human labor must be introduced into the social organism in a manner which does not disturb the worker's sense of human dignity will only result from observing the relation which human labor has to the development of individual capabilities on the one hand and to rights-awareness on the other.

People are asking today — and rightly so — what is the first step to be taken in order to satisfy the demands which are arising in the social movement. Even the first step will not be taken in a worthwhile manner if it is not known what relation this step should have to the foundations of a healthy social organism. One who knows this will be able to find the appropriate tasks wherever he happens to be, or wherever he decides to go. Acquisition of the insight referred to here has been prevented by what has passed over, during a long period of time, from human will into social institutions. People have become so accustomed to these institutions that their views about what should be preserved in them and what should be changed in them is determined by the institutions themselves. Their thoughts conform to the things, instead of mastering them. It is necessary today to perceive that it is only possible to arrive at factual judgments through a return to the fundamental thoughts which are the basis for all social institutions.

If adequate sources are not present from which the forces that reside in these fundamental thoughts constantly flow into the social organism, then the institutions take on forms which inhibit rather than further life. The fundamental thoughts live on, more or less unconsciously, in human instinctive impulses however, while fully conscious thoughts lead to error and create hindrances to life. These fundamental thoughts, which manifest themselves chaotically in a life inhibiting world, are what underlie, openly or disguised, the revolutionary convulsions of the social organism. These convulsions will not occur once the social organism is structured in such a way that the tendency is prevalent to observe at what point institutions diverge from the forms indicated by the fundamental thoughts, and to counteract such divergences before they become dangerously powerful.

In our times, divergences from the conditions required by the fundamental thoughts have become great in many aspects of human life. The living impulse of these thoughts stands in human souls as a vocal criticism, through events, of the form the social organism has assumed during the last centuries. Good will is therefore necessary in order to turn energetically to the fundamental thoughts and not to underestimate how damaging it is, especially today, to banish them from life as impractical generalities. Criticism of what modern times have made of the social organism exists in the life and in the demands of the proletarian population. The task of our times is to counteract the one-sided criticism by finding, in the fundamental thoughts, the direction to be taken in order that events be consciously guided. For the time is gone in which humanity can be satisfied with what instinctive guidance is able to achieve.

One of the basic questions that has developed in contemporary criticism is how to put an end to the oppression which proletarian humanity has experienced through private capitalism. The owner, or manager, of capital is in a position to put the physical labor of other people at the service of whatever he undertakes to produce. It is necessary to differentiate between three sectors in the social relationship which arises through the cooperation of capital and human labor: the managerial activity, which must be based upon the individual abilities of a person or a group of persons; the relationship of the manager to the worker, which must be a legal one; the production of an article which acquires commodity value in economic circulation. Managerial activity can only participate soundly in the social organism when forces are active in this organism which allow individual human abilities to manifest themselves in the best possible manner. This can only occur if there is a sector of the social organism which allows capable individuals free initiative to exercise their abilities and enables the evaluation of these abilities to be made through the free understanding of others. It is evident that the social activity of a person utilizing capital belongs in the sector of the social organism in which spiritual life provides the laws and administration. Should the political state participate in this activity, then a lack of appreciation of the effectiveness of individual abilities must necessarily become a co-determining factor. The political state must be based upon, and occupy itself with, those requirements which are common and equal to all. It must, in its area, ensure that each individual is able to assert his opinion. The appreciation or non-appreciation of individual abilities is not one of its functions. Therefore, what takes place within its framework may not influence the exercise of individual human abilities. Nor should the prospect of economic profit be the determining factor in the exercise of individual abilities through the use of capital. Many critics of capitalism lay particular stress on this economic profit factor. They assume that individual abilities can only be actuated by this incentive. As 'practical' people, they refer to 'imperfect' human nature, which they pretend to know. It is true that, within the social order which contemporary conditions have occasioned, the prospect of profit has attained enormous importance. But this fact is no less the cause of the conditions which are now being experienced. These conditions call urgently for the development of some other motivation for the actuation of individual abilities. This motivation will have to be found in the social understanding which issues from a healthy spiritual life. With the strength of free spiritual life the schools, education will equip the individual with impulses which, by virtue of this inherent understanding, will enable him to put his personal abilities into practice.

This opinion is by no means fantastic. Certainly fantastic notions have caused as much damage in the field of social will as in any other. But the view expressed here, as can be seen from the foregoing, is not based upon the delusion that 'the spirit' will work wonders if only those who think they are endowed with some. talk as much as possible about it; it is rather the result of observing the free cooperation of human beings in spiritual fields of endeavor This cooperation, when it is able to develop in a truly free manner, acquires, through its own essence, a social form.

Only the unfree kind of spiritual life has, until now, prevented this social form from emerging. Spiritual strength has been cultivated within the ruling classes in a way that has antisocially restricted its achievements to these classes. What was accomplished within these classes could only be transmitted artificially to proletarian humanity. And this part of humanity could draw no soul-sustaining strength from spiritual life because it did not really participate in these spiritual values. Institutes of popular adult education, leading the people to an appreciation of art, and similar actions, are not really valid means for the propagation of spiritual values as long as these spiritual values retain the character they have taken on in recent times. The innermost human essence is not to be found in such values. The working classes can therefore only look on from an outside observation point. What holds true in respect of spiritual life proper is also the case with the ramifications of spiritual activity which flow into economic life along with capital. In a healthy social organism the proletarian worker should not merely stand at his machine concerned with nothing but its operation, while the capitalist alone knows the fate of the produced commodities in economic circulation. Through fully active participation the worker should be able to develop a clear idea of his own involvement in society through his work on the production of commodities. Regular discussions, which must be considered to be as much a part of the operation as the work itself, should be arranged by management with a view to developing ideas which circumscribe employer and employed alike. A healthy activity of this kind will result in an understanding by the worker that correct management of capital benefits the social organism and therewith the worker himself. By means of such openness, based on free mutual understanding, the entrepreneur will be induced to conduct his business in an irreproachable manner.

Only someone who cannot sense the social effect of a common undertaking's united inner experience will hold what has been said here to be meaningless. Someone who can sense this effect will see how economic productivity is stimulated when the capital-based management of economic life has its roots in the free spiritual sector. The interest in capital for the purpose of making and increasing profits can only be replaced by an objective interest in the production of commodities and in achievement if this prerequisite is met.

The socialistic minded strive for the administration of the means of production by the state. What is justified in their efforts can only be attained when this administration becomes the responsibility of the spiritual sector. The economic coercion which the capitalist exercises when he develops his activities from the forces of economic life will thereby become impossible. And the paralyzing of individual human abilities, as is the case when these abilities are administered by the political state, cannot occur.

The proceeds from the use of capital and individual human abilities must derive, as is the case with all spiritual effort, from the free initiative of the doer on one side, and the free recognition by those others who require his efforts on the other. The determination of the amount of these proceeds must be in agreement with the doer's own free insight into what is suitable, taking into consideration his preparation, expenditures, and so forth. His claims in this respect will be satisfied only when his efforts are met with recognition.

Through the kind of social arrangements described here, the ground can be prepared for a truly free contractual relationship between manager and worker. This does not mean an exchange of commodities, i.e. money, for labor-power, but an agreement as to the share each of the persons who jointly produced the product is to receive.

What is achieved for the social organism with capital as its basis depends, by its very nature, on how individual human abilities intervene in this organism. The corresponding impulse for the development of these abilities can only be obtained through a free spiritual life. In a social organism in which the development of these abilities is harnessed to a political state or to the economy, the real productivity of everything requiring the expenditure of capital depends upon free individual forces overcoming these paralyzing conditions. But development under such conditions is unsound. Free deployment of individual abilities in the use of capital has not been the cause of conditions in which labor has become a commodity; the fettering of these abilities by the political state or economic interests is responsible for these conditions. Unprejudiced comprehension of this fact is a prerequisite for everything which should come about in the field of social organization. Modern times have produced the superstition that the means for making the social organism healthy can emerge from the political state or the economic sector. If humanity continues in the direction indicated by this superstition, social institutions will be created which will not lead humanity to what it strives for, but to an unlimited increase in the oppression which it seeks to avert.

People began thinking about capitalism at a time when it was seen as the cause of a deterioration in the social organism. One experiences this deterioration and sees that it must be fought against. It is necessary to see more. One must become aware that the illness has its origin in the draining of the effective forces in capital by the economic process. Only by avoiding the illusion caused by the manner of thinking which sees the management of capital by a liberated spiritual sector as the result of 'impractical idealism,' is it possible to work in the direction which the evolutionary forces of contemporary humanity are beginning to demand.

Certainly people are poorly prepared at the present time to directly relate the social ideas, which are to guide capitalism along a healthy course, with spiritual life. Only economic life is taken into consideration. It is easily seen how, in modern times, commodity production has led to large-scale industrial enterprises, and this in turn to the contemporary form of capitalism. Cooperatives, which work to satisfy the needs of the producers, are supposed to take the place of this economic form. Since modern means of production are obviously to be retained however, the concentration of all enterprises in one great cooperative is called for. In such a system, it is thought, each person would produce on behalf of the community, which could not be exploitative because it would be exploiting itself. And because one must, or wants to, relate to what already exists, one looks to the modern state, which is to be transformed into an all-embracing cooperative.

It is not realized that what is expected of such a cooperative is less likely to occur the larger it becomes. If the integration of individual human abilities into the cooperative organism is not structured as described here, then the common management of labor cannot lead to the social organism's recovery.

The present meager inclination toward an unbiased judgment as far as the intervention of spiritual life in the social organism is concerned, is the result of people having become accustomed to imagine the spiritual as being as far removed as possible from everything which is material and practical. They will not be few who will find something grotesque in the view expressed here, that the actuation of capital in economic life should partially manifest the effects of the spiritual sector. One can well imagine that the members of the hitherto ruling classes are in agreement with socialist thinkers on this point.

In order to recognize the importance for the recovery of the social organism of what they consider grotesque, one must direct one's attention to certain contemporary currents of thought which, in their way, derive from honest impulses of the soul, but hinder the development of real social thinking wherever they find entry.

These currents of thought flow — more or less unconsciously — away from what gives inner experience the right impulse. They strive after a philosophy and an inner life of the soul and intellect which accords with the search for scientific knowledge, but which is like an island in the sea of human existence. They are not able to build a bridge from that life to the everyday life of reality. One can see how many people nowadays find it fashionable to reflect, in their ivory towers, in scholastic abstractions on all kinds of ethical-religious problems; one can see how people reflect on how man can acquire virtues, how he should behave lovingly toward his fellow-men, and how he can become inspired with an inner meaning of life. But one also sees the impossibility of realizing a carry-over from what people call good and loving and benevolent and right and moral to what surrounds humanity in everyday external reality in the form of capital, of labor remuneration, of consumption, of production, of commodity circulation, of credit, of banks and stock markets. One can see how two universal currents also flow alongside each other in human thought-habits. One current is that which remains at divine-spiritual heights, so to speak, and has no desire to build bridges between what constitutes a spiritual impulse and the realities of the ordinary dealings of life. The other lives, devoid of thought, in everyday life. Life, however, is a unity. It can only prosper if the strength from ethical-religious life works down into the commonplace, profane life, into that life which, to many, may seem less fashionable. For if one fails to erect a bridge between these two aspects, one falls into mere fantasy, far removed from true everyday reality as far as religious and moral life and social thinking are concerned. These true everyday realities then have their revenge. From out of a certain spiritual impulse man strives towards all kinds of ideals, towards what he calls good; but he devotes himself without spirit to those other instincts based on the ordinary daily necessities of life which must be satisfied through economic activities. He knows of no practicable way from the concept of spirituality to what goes on in everyday life. Therefore this life takes on a form having nothing to do with ethical impulses, which remain at fashionable, spiritual heights. But then the revenge of the commonplace is such that the ethical-religious life constitutes an inner lie, for it remains at a distance from the commonplace, out of direct contact with practical life, without this fact even being perceived.

How many people there are nowadays who, through ethical-religious high-mindedness, demonstrate the best will to live correctly together with their fellow-men, wishing them only the very best. They fail, however, to adopt the necessary sensibilities, for they cannot acquire the concrete social concepts which affect the practical conduct of life.

It is people such as these, fantasists who think they are practical, who in this historical moment when the social questions have become so urgent, hinder all real progress. One can hear them speak as follows: 'It is necessary for humanity to rise up from materialism, from the external material life which has driven us into the catastrophe of the world-war, and turn to a spiritual conception of life.' In order to show the path to spirituality, they never tire of citing the personalities of the past who were venerated for their spiritual way of thinking. If, however, one tries to indicate what the spirit must necessarily accomplish today in practical life, how daily bread must be produced, it is immediately contended that first of all people must be brought to once again acknowledge the spirit. But the heart of the matter today is that the guidelines for the recovery of the social organism are to be found in the strength of spiritual life. For this it is not sufficient that people occupy themselves with the spirit as a sideline. For this it is necessary that everyday life become spiritually oriented. The tendency to treat spiritual life as a sideline has led the hitherto ruling classes to acquire a taste for social conditions which have resulted in the current state of affairs.

In contemporary society, management of capital for the production of commodities is closely allied to the possession of the means of production, which is also capital. Nevertheless, these two relationships of man to capital are quite different as far as their effects within the social organism are concerned. Management through individual abilities, when they are properly exercised, supplies the social organism with goods in which everyone who belongs to this organism has an interest. Whatever a person's situation in life, it is in his interest that nothing be lost of what flows from the sources of human nature in the form of individual abilities, by means of which the goods are produced that purposefully serve human life. The development of these abilities can only ensue when their possessors are able to activate them with their own free initiative. The welfare of humanity is, at least to a certain extent, deprived of whatever is not able to flow from these sources in freedom. Capital is the means by which such abilities are made effective for wide areas of the social organism. Everyone within a social organism must have a real interest in the sum total of capital being managed in such a way that particularly gifted individuals or groups have this capital at the disposal of their own free initiative. Every person, whether his work is spiritually creative or that of a laborer, if he wishes to objectively serve his own interests, would like a sufficiently large number of competent persons or groups of persons not only to have capital freely at their disposal, but also that it become accessible to them through their own initiative. For only they can judge how their individual abilities, through the mediation of capital, will purposefully produce goods for the social organism.

It is not necessary to describe within the framework of this book how, in the course of human evolution, private ownership developed out of other forms of ownership in connection with the activation of individual human abilities. In recent times, ownership has developed within the social organism under the influence of the division of labor We are concerned here with contemporary conditions and their necessary further development.

However private ownership may have arisen, through the exercise of power, conquest and so forth, it is a result of social creation bound to individual human abilities. Nevertheless, the current opinion of the socialists is that the oppressive nature of private ownership can only be done away with through its transformation into common ownership. The question is put so: How can the private ownership of the means of production be prevented in order that the resulting oppression of the unpropertied cease? Whoever puts the question in this way overlooks the fact that the social organism is constantly becoming and growing. It is not possible to ask how something that grows should be organized in order that this organization, which is thought to be correct, be preserved into the future. One can think in this way about something which remains unchanged from its beginnings. But it is not valid for the social organism. As a living entity it is constantly changing whatever arises within it. To attempt to give it a supposedly best form, in which it is expected to remain, is to undermine its vitality.

One of the conditions of the social organism is that those who can serve the community through their individual abilities should not be deprived of using their free initiative. Where such service requires that the means of production be freely at their disposal, the hindering of this free initiative would only be harmful to the general social interest. The usual argument, that the entrepreneur needs the prospect of profit as an incentive and that this profit is closely related to ownership of the means of production, is rejected here. The kind of thinking from which the opinions expressed in this book derive, that there is a further evolution of social conditions, must see in the liberation of spiritual life from the political and economic sectors the possibility that this form of incentive can cease to exist.

Liberated spiritual life will, necessarily, develop social understanding, and from this understanding will result quite different forms of incentive than the hope of economic advantage. However, it is not a question of which impulses arouse sympathy for private ownership of the means of production, but whether the free disposition of these means or that disposition which is regulated by the community is what corresponds to the vital needs of the social organism. Moreover, it must always be kept in mind that the conditions which are thought to be observed in primitive human societies are not applicable to the contemporary social organism; only those conditions which correspond to today's stage of development are applicable.

At this present stage, a fertile activation of individual abilities cannot be introduced into the economic process without free disposition over capital. If production is to be fruitful, this disposition must be possible, not because it is advantageous to an individual or a group of individuals, but because, when utilized with the proper social understanding, it can best serve the community.

The human being relates to what he produces, alone or together with others, as he relates to the dexterity of his own limbs. The undermining of free disposition over the means of production is equivalent to crippling the free application of dexterity in his limbs.

Private ownership is, however, nothing other than the medium for this free disposition. As far as the social organism is concerned, the only significance of ownership is that the owner has the right of disposition over the property through his own free initiative. One sees that in society two things are bound together which have quite different significance for the social organism: the free disposition over the capital base of social production, and the legal relationship through which he who exercises this disposition, by means of his right of disposition, precludes others from the free utilization of this capital base.

It is not the original free disposition which leads to social damage, but only the prolongation of the right of disposition when the appropriate conditions which connect individual human abilities to this disposition have ceased to exist. Whoever sees the social organism as something evolving, growing, will not misunderstand what is indicated here. He will seek possibilities whereby that which serves life can be administered so that its effects will not be harmful. What lives cannot be fruitfully established without disadvantages occurring during the process of becoming. And should one work on an evolving entity, as man must on the social organism, then the task may not be to hinder a necessary facility in order to avoid damage, for then one would undermine the possibilities for life of the social organism. It is a matter of intervening at the right moment, when what has been appropriate is about to become harmful.

The possibility of free disposition over the capital base through individual abilities must exist; it must be possible to change the related property rights as soon as they become a means for the unjustified acquisition of power. We do have a facility which partially fulfills this requirement in respect of so-called intellectual property. At a certain time after its creator's death it becomes community property. This corresponds to a truly social way of thinking. Closely as the creation of a purely intellectual property is bound to an individual's talents, it is at the same time a product of human society and must, at the right moment, be handed over to this society. It is in no way different with respect to other property. That which the individual produces in the service of the community is only possible in cooperation with this community. The right of disposition over a property cannot be administered separate from the community's interests. A means of eliminating the ownership of the capital base is not to be sought, but rather a means of administering this property so that it best serves the community.

This means can be found in the threefold social organism. The people, united in the social organism, act as a totality through the rights-state. The exercise of individual abilities pertains to the spiritual organization.

Everything in the social organism, when viewed realistically and without subjective opinions, theories, desires and so forth, indicates the necessity for the threefold formation of the social organism. This is particularly true as regards the relation of individual human abilities to the capital base of economic life and the ownership of this capital base. The rights-state will not have to prevent the formation and administration of privately owned capital as long as individual abilities remain bound to the capital base in a way that constitutes a service to the whole of the social organism. Furthermore, it will remain a rights-state in regard to private property, never making private property its own, but ensuring that rights of disposition are transferred at the right moment to a person or a group of persons capable of restoring the appropriate individual relationship to the property. The social organism will thereby be served from two completely different angles. The democratic rights state, which is concerned with what affects all people in an equal manner, will guard against property rights becoming property wrongs. Because this state does not itself administer property, but ensures its transfer to individual human abilities, these abilities will develop their productive powers for the totality of the social organism. Through such organization, property rights, or the disposition over them, may retain a personal element as long as seems opportune. One can imagine that the representatives in the rights-state will, at different times, enact completely different laws concerning the transference of property from one person, or group of persons, to others. At the present time, when a great mistrust of all private property is widespread, a radical transference of private property to community [state] property is contemplated. Should this way be followed, it will be seen to impair the vital potentialities of the social organism. Taught by experience, another way will then be taken. It would, however, doubtless be better if arrangements were undertaken now which would, in the sense indicated here, bestow health on the social organism. As long as a person alone, or in connection with a group, continues the productive activity which procured for him a capital base, his right of disposition over the capital accumulation which results from operating profits on original capital will have to remain in effect when it is used for an expansion of production. From the moment such a person ceases to manage production, this capital accumulation should pass to another person, or group of persons, to be utilized for the same or some other type of production which serves the social organism. Capital gains which are not used for expansion should be similarly treated. The only thing personally owned by the individual who operates an enterprise should be what he receives in accordance with the terms agreed to when he takes over responsibility for production, and which he feels are appropriate to his individual abilities; and which, furthermore, seem justified by the confidence of others in granting him the use of capital. Should the capital be increased through the activities of this individual, then he would be entitled to a portion of the increase, which would correspond to an interest-like percentage. When the first administrator no longer can or will manage an enterprise, the capital with which it was established will either be transferred to a new administrator, along with all obligations or, depending on the wishes of the original owners, be returned to them.

Such arrangements concern the transference of rights. The legal provisions by which these transfers are to take place are the province of the rights-state. It will also have to see to their execution and administration. One can safely assume that the detailed determinations which regulate such transfers will vary according to what rights-awareness considers correct. A realistic way of thinking will never desire more than to point out the direction that such regulation can take. If this direction is taken with understanding, the appropriate action for specific individual cases can always be found. The correct solution will always have to be in accordance with the spirit of the thing as well as whatever special conditions practical considerations may impose. The more realistic a way of thinking is, the less it will seek to establish laws and rules from predetermined requirements. On the other hand, the spirit of such a way of thinking will necessarily lead to certain requirements. One such result will be that the rights-state will never take over the disposition of capital through its administration of transfer rights. It has only to provide for the transfer to a person or group of persons whose individual abilities seem to warrant it. In general, it follows that it should at first be possible for someone who proposes to effect such a capital transference under the circumstances described to freely choose his successor. He will be able to choose a person, or group of persons, or transfer the disposition rights to an establishment of the spiritual organization. A person who has purposefully served the social organism through the management of capital will determine the future use of this capital with social understanding derived from his individual abilities. Furthermore, it will be more advantageous for the social organism to depend upon this determination than to dispense with it and have settlements made by people not directly concerned with the matter.

Settlements of this kind will pertain to capital accumulations exceeding a certain amount which are acquired by a person or group through the use of means of production (to which real estate also belongs), and which are not included in what Is originally agreed upon as compensation for the activities of individual abilities.

Such earnings, acquisitions and savings which result from the individual's own work will remain in his personal possession until his death, or in his descendants' possession until a later date. Until this date interest (the amount of which is to be determined from rights-awareness and set by the rights state) will be paid by whoever receives such savings for the procurement of means of production. In a social order based upon the principles described herein, it will be possible to completely separate the proceeds which result from the use of means of production from assets acquired by means of personal (physical and mental) work. This separation accords with rights-awareness as well as the Interests of the social community. What someone saves and makes available for production serves the general interest, for it makes the management of production through individual human abilities possible in the first place. Capital increase through the use of means of production – after the deduction of legitimate interest – owes its development to the overall social organism. It should therefore also flow back into it in the way described. The rights-state has only to ensure that the transference of the capital in question takes place in the manner indicated; it will not be incumbent upon it to decide which material or spiritual production is to have disposition over transferred capital or over savings. That would lead to a tyranny of the state over spiritual and material production, which is best administered through individual human abilities. In case someone does not wish to personally select the receiver of capital accumulated by him, he will be able to delegate this function to a unit of the spiritual organization.

After the death of the earner, or at a certain time thereafter, assets acquired through savings, along with the corresponding interest, also go to a spiritually or materially productive person or group – but only to such a person or group and not to an unproductive person in whose hands it would constitute a private pension – to be chosen by the earner and specified in his will). Here again, if a person or group cannot be chosen directly, the transfer of disposition rights to an establishment of the spiritual organism will come into consideration. Only if someone does not himself effect a disposition will the rights-state step in and, through the spiritual organization, make the disposition for him.

In a social order arranged in this way the initiative of the individual as well as the interests of the social community are taken into account. Indeed, such interests are fully satisfied by individual initiatives being placed at their service. Under such an arrangement, someone who entrusts his labor to the guidance of another will know that the results of their joint efforts will serve the community, and therewith the worker himself, in the best possible way. The social order meant here will create a healthy, sensible relationship between capital, as embodied in means of production, together with human labor on the one hand, and the prices of the articles produced by them on the other. Perhaps imperfections are contained in what is presented here. Then let them be found. It is not the function of a way of thinking which corresponds to reality to formulate perfect programs for all time, but to point out the direction for practical work. The intention of the specific examples mentioned here is to better illustrate the indicated direction. A productive goal can still be attained as long as improvements coincide with the direction given.

Justified personal or family interests will be brought into concordance with the requirements of the human community through such arrangements. It is of course possible to point out that there will be a strong temptation to pass on property to one or more descendants during the original owner's lifetime. Also, that although descendants could be made to look like producers, they would nevertheless be inefficient compared to others who should replace them. This temptation could be reduced to a minimum in an organization governed by the arrangements described above. The rights-state has only to require that under all circumstances property transferred from one family member to another must, upon the lapse of a certain period of time after the death of the former, devolve upon an establishment of the spiritual organization. Or evasion of the rule can be prevented in some other way through the law. The rights-state will only insure that the transfer takes place; a facility of the spiritual organization should determine who is to receive the inheritance. Through the fulfillment of these principles an awareness will develop of the necessity for offspring being made qualified for the social organism through education and training, and of the socially harmful results of transferring capital to unproductive persons. Someone who is really imbued with social understanding will have no interest in his relation to a capital base passing to a person or group whose individual abilities do not justify it.

No one with a sense for the truly practicable will consider what is presented here as utopian. The only arrangements proposed are those which can develop in accordance with contemporary conditions in all walks of life. It is only necessary to decide once and for all that the rights-state must gradually relinquish its control over spiritual-cultural life and the economy, and not to offer resistance when what should happen really happens: that private educational institutions arise and the economy becomes self-sustaining. The state-owned schools and economic enterprises do not have to be eliminated overnight, but the gradual dismantling of the state educational and economic apparatus could well develop from small beginnings. Above all, it is necessary for those who are thoroughly convinced of the correctness of these or similar social ideas to provide for their dissemination. If these ideas find understanding, confidence will arise in the possibility of a healthy transformation of present conditions into others which are not harmful. This is the only confidence that can bring about a really healthy evolution, for whoever would acquire this confidence must perceive how new institutions could be practically merged with existing ones. The essential element of the ideas developed here is that they do not advocate the advent of a better future through even greater destruction of society than has already occurred, but that the realization of such ideas is to come about by building upon what already exists. Through this building, the dismantling of the unhealthy elements is induced. Explanations which do not instill confidence of this sort cannot attain what absolutely must be attained: a course in which the value of what has hitherto been produced, and the abilities which have been acquired, are not simply thrown overboard, but are preserved. Even those who think in a very radical way can acquire confidence in a new social structure which carries over existing values if the ideas which accompany it are capable of introducing truly healthy developments. Even they must realize that, regardless of which social class attains power, it will not be able to eliminate the existing evils if its impulses are not supported by ideas which make the social organism healthy and viable. To despair because one does not believe that a sufficiently large number of people, even in the present troubled circumstances, can find understanding for such ideas even if sufficient energy is dedicated to their dissemination, is to despair of human nature's susceptibility to purposeful and health-giving impulses. This question, whether one should despair or not, should not be asked, rather only this: How can ideas which instill confidence be explained in the most effective possible way?

An effective dissemination of the ideas presented here will meet opposition from the thought-habits of contemporary times on two grounds. Either it will be argued that to tear asunder uniform society is not possible because the three sectors which have been described are, in reality, interrelated at all social levels; or that the necessary autonomous character of each of the three sectors can also be attained in the uniform state, and that what is presented here is no more than a fantasy The first objection unrealistically supposes that unity can only be achieved in a community by means of directives. Reality, however, demands the opposite.

Unity must arise as the result of activities streaming together from various directions. The developments of recent years have run counter to this reality. Furthermore, what lives in human beings has resisted the order brought into their lives from without, which has led to the present state of affairs.

The second prejudice results from an inability to perceive the radical difference in function inherent In the three sectors of society. It is not seen how the human being has a special relation to each of the three sectors, each one separate from the other two but cooperating with them, on which this relation can take form. According to the physiocratic theory of the past, either governments take measures concerning economic life which are in contradiction to its self-development, in which case such measures are harmful; or the laws coincide with the direction economic life takes when it is left alone, in which case they are superfluous. Academically, this view is antiquated; as thought-habit however, it still devastatingly haunts people's brains. It is thought that if one sector of life follows its own laws, then everything necessary for life must arise from this sector. If, for example, economic life were regulated in a way that people found satisfactory, then the appropriate rights and spiritual sectors would also result from this orderly economic foundation. But this is not possible, and only thinking which is foreign to reality can believe that it is possible. There is nothing in the economic sector to provide the motivation necessary to regulate what derives from the rights-awareness of a person-to-person relationship. If this relationship is regulated according to economic motivation, then the human being, together with his labor and with the disposition over the means to labor, is harnessed to economic life. He becomes a cog, a mechanism of the economic system. Economic life tends to move in one direction only, and this must be compensated for from another side. Legal measures are not necessarily good when they follow the direction determined by the economy, nor are they necessarily harmful when they run counter to it; rather, when the direction of economic life is continually influenced by the law, in its application to human beings as such, an existence worthy of humanity will be introduced into economic life. Furthermore, only when individual abilities are completely separated from economic life, when they grow on their own foundation and unceasingly supply economic life with the strength which it cannot produce within itself, will it be able to develop in a manner which is beneficial to humanity.

It is noteworthy that in everyday life one easily sees the advantage of the division of labor. One does not expect a tailor to keep his own cow in order to have milk. As far as the comprehensive formation of human life is concerned however, one believes that only a uniform structure can be useful.

It is inevitable that social ideas which correspond to reality will give rise to objections from all sides, for life breeds contradictions. He who thinks realistically will seek to institute facilities the contradictions of which are compensated for by other facilities. He may not believe that a facility which to his mind is ideally good will, when put into practice, be without contradictions. Contemporary socialism is thoroughly justified when it demands that the modern facilities which produce profits for individuals be replaced by others which produce for the consumption of all. However, the person who fully recognizes this demand cannot come to modern socialism's conclusion: that the means of production must pass from private ownership to common state ownership. Rather, he will come to a quite different conclusion: that what is privately produced through individual competence must be made available to the community in the correct way. The impulse of modern industry has been to create income through the mass production of goods. The task of the future will be to find, through associations, the kind of production which most accords with the needs of consumers and the most appropriate channels from the producers to the consumers. Legal arrangements will ensure that a productive enterprise remains connected to a person or group only as long as the connection is justified by their individual abilities. Instead of common ownership of the means of production, a circulation of these means – continually putting them at the disposal of the persons whose individual abilities can best employ them for the benefit of the community – will be introduced into the social organism. In this way the connection between individuality and means of production, hitherto effected through private ownership, is established on a temporary basis. The manager and sub-managers of an enterprise will have the means of production to thank for the fact that their abilities can provide them with the income they require. They will not fail to make production as efficient as possible, for an increase in production, although not bringing them the full profit, does provide them with a portion of the proceeds. As described above, the profit goes to the community only after an interest has been deducted and credited to the producer due to the increase in production. It is also in the spirit of what is presented here that when production falls off the producer's income is to diminish in the same measure as it increases with an expansion of production. Additional income will always result from the manager's mental achievement, and not from the forces inherent in community cooperation.

Through the realization of such social ideas as are presented here, the institutions which exist today will acquire a completely new significance. The ownership of property ceases to be what it has been until now. Nor is an obsolete form reinstated, as would be the case with common ownership, but an advance to something completely new is made. The objects of ownership are introduced into the flux of social life. They cannot be administered by a private individual for his private interests to the detriment of the community, but neither will the community be able to administer them bureaucratically to the detriment of the individual. Rather will the suitable individual have access to them in order therewith to serve the community.

A sense for the common interest can develop through the realization of impulses that put production on a sound basis and safeguard the social organism from the dangers of crises. Also, a management which only occupies itself with economic processes will be able to carry out the necessary adjustments. For example, should a company which is fulfilling a need not be in a position to pay its creditors the interest due them on their savings, other companies, in free agreement with all concerned, could make up whatever is lacking. A self-contained economic process which receives both its legal basis and a continuous supply of individual human abilities from outside itself will be able to restrict its activities to the economic sector. It will therefore occasion a distribution of goods which will ensure that each receives what he is entitled to in accordance with the community's welfare. If one person appears to have more income than another, this will only be because this 'more' benefits the community due to his individual abilities.

In a social organism which functions in accordance with the manner of thinking presented here, the contributions necessary for the upkeep of rights institutions will be arranged through agreement between the leaders of the rights sector and the economic sector. Everything necessary for the maintenance of the spiritual organization, including remuneration, will come to it through the free appreciation of the individuals who participate in the social organism. A sound basis for the spiritual organization will result from free competition among the individuals capable of spiritual work.

Only in a social organism of the kind described here will the rights administration be able to acquire the understanding necessary for a just distribution of goods. An economic organism which does not lay claim to human labor according to the needs of the various branches of production, but which has to operate in accordance with what the law allows, will determine the worth of commodities according to the work of the men who produce them. Commodity values, which are unrelated to human welfare and dignity, will not determine human work-performance. Rights in such an organism will result from purely human relations. Children will have the right to education; the working head of a family will have a higher income than a single person. The 'more' will come to him through arrangements established by agreement of all three social organizations. The right to education could be arranged in that the economic organization's administration, in accordance with the general economic situation, calculates the amount of educational income possible, while the rights-state, in consultation with the spiritual organization, determines the rights of the individual in this respect. Once again, this indication is meant as an example of the direction in which arrangements can be made. It is possible that quite different arrangements would be appropriate in specific cases. However, they can only be found through the purposeful cooperation of the three autonomous members of the social organism. Contrary to what often passes for practical today but is not, this presentation wishes to find the truly practical, namely, a formation of the social organism which enables people to strive for what is socially desirable. Just as children have the right to an education, the elderly, the infirm and widows have the right to a decent maintenance. The necessary capital must be provided for in the same way that it is for the education of those who are not yet productive. The essential point of all this is that the income of the non-earners Is not determined by the economic sector; on the contrary, the economic sector becomes dependent upon the results of rights-awareness. Those who work

In an economic organism will receive that much less from the results of their work as more flows to the non-earners. However, this 'less' will be borne equally by all participants in the social organism if the social impulse described here is realized. The education and support of those who are incapable of working is something which concerns all humanity, and, through a rights-state detached from the economy, it will be so, for every individual who is of age will have a voice in the rights-organization.

In a social organism which corresponds to the manner of thinking characterized here, a person's surplus performance, made possible by his individual abilities, will be passed on to the community just as the legitimate support for the deficit performance of the less capable will be drawn from this same community. 'Surplus value' will not be created for the enjoyment of individuals, but for the increased supply of intellectual or material wealth to the social organism; and for the cultivation of what is produced within this organism but which is not of immediate use to it.

Whoever is of the opinion that keeping the three sectors of the social organism apart would only have an ideal value, and that this condition would come about 'of itself' in a uniformly structured state organism or in an economic cooperative which Includes the state and is based on the common ownership of means of production, should direct his attention to the special kind of social facilities which must result from a realization of the threefold formation. The legitimacy of money as a means of payment, for example, would no longer be the responsibility of the government, but would depend upon measures taken by the administrative bodies of the economic organization. Money, in an healthy social organism, can be nothing other than a draft on commodities produced by others, which the holder may claim from the overall social organism because he has himself produced and delivered commodities to this sector. An economic sector becomes a uniform economy through the circulation of money. Each produces for all on the roundabout path of economic life. The economic sector is only concerned with commodity values. Activities which originate in the spiritual or state organizations also take on a commodity character for this sector. A teacher's activity with respect to his pupils is, for the economic process, of a commodity nature. A teacher is no more paid for his individual abilities than the worker is paid for his labor-power. It is only possible to pay for what they both produce as commodities for the economic process. How free initiative and the law should contribute to the production of commodities lies just as much outside the economic process as the effects of the forces of nature on the grain yield in a bountiful or in a lean year. As far as the economic process is concerned the spiritual organization, in respect to its economic requirements, and also the state, are simply commodity producers. What they produce within their own sectors are not commodities however; they only become such once they enter into the economic process. Their activities are not commercial within their own sectors; the economic organism's management carries on its commercial activities using the achievements of the other sectors.

The purely economic value of a commodity (or service), in so far as it is expressed in the money which represents its equivalent value, will be dependent upon the efficiency with which economic management functions. The development of economic productivity will depend upon the measures taken by this management, with its spiritual and legal foundation provided by the other two members of the social organism. The monetary value of a commodity will then express the fact that the facilities of the economic organism are producing these commodities in an amount which corresponds to the need for them. Should the suggestions contained in this book be realized, then the economic impulse to accumulate wealth through sheer quantity of production will no longer be decisive; rather will the associations adapt the production of goods to actual need. In this way a need-oriented relation between monetary values and the production facilities in the economic organism will develop. In the healthy social organism money will really only be a measure of value, since commodity production, the only means through which the possessor of money will have been able to attain it, will back every coin and bank note. Due to the nature of these relations, arrangements will have to be made whereby money loses its value for its possessor once it has lost this significance. Such arrangements have already been alluded to. Property in the form of money passes on to the community after a certain length of time. In order to prevent money which is not working in productive enterprises being retained through evasion of the economic organization's measures, a new printing could take place from time to time. One result of such measures is that the interest derived from capital would diminish in the course of time. Money will wear out, just as commodities wear out. Nevertheless, such a measure will be a just and appropriate one for the state to enact. There cannot be any 'interest on interest.' Whoever has accumulated savings has surely also rendered services which entitle him to claim reciprocal services in the form of commodities, just as present day efforts give claim to reciprocal efforts; but these claims are subject to limits, for claims originating in the past can only be satisfied by performance in the present. They may not be allowed to turn into means of economic power. Through the realization of these conditions, the currency question is given a healthy foundation. Regardless of what form money takes due to other considerations, currency as such depends on the rational administration of the overall social organism. No political state will ever solve the currency question in a satisfactory manner by making laws.

Contemporary states will only solve it by renouncing their efforts at reaching a solution and leaving the necessary measures to an autonomous economic organism.

Much has been said about the modern division of labor, about its time-saving effects, its contribution to perfecting the production process and the exchange of commodities, etc., but little attention has been paid to how it influences the individual's relation to his work performance. Whoever works in a social organism which is based on the division of labor never really earns his income by himself; he earns it through the work of all the participants in the social organism. A tailor who makes his own coat does not do so in the same sense as a person living in a primitive society who must provide for all his necessities himself. He makes the coat in order to be able to make clothes for others; and the coat's value for him depends on the others' work performance. The coat is actually a means of production. Some would call this hair-splitting. They cannot, however, continue to hold this opinion as soon as they observe how commodity values form in the economic process. They then see that it is not even possible to work for oneself in an economic organism based on the division of labor One can only work for others, and let others work for oneself. One can no more work for oneself than one can devour oneself. Arrangements may be made which are in contradiction to the principle of the division of labor however. This occurs when goods are produced merely in order to turn over to an individual as property what he is able to produce only because of his position in the social organism. The division of labor exerts pressure on the social organism which has the effect of causing the individual in it to live according to the conditions prevalent in the overall organism; economically, it precludes egotism. Should egotism be present nevertheless in the form of class privilege and the like, an untenable situation arises which leads to severe disturbances in the social organism. We are living under such conditions today. There may well be many people who think little of a demand that the law and other facilities conform to the egotism-free working of the division of labor They should then realize the consequences of this attitude: that one can do nothing at all; the social movement will lead to nothing. One can certainly do nothing with this movement without respecting reality. The manner of thinking from which the writing of this book is derived intends that the human being strive toward what is necessary for the life of the social organism.

Someone who can only form concepts in accordance with customary practices will be uneasy when he hears that labor-management relations should be disengaged from the economic organism. He will believe that such a disengagement would necessarily lead to currency devaluation and a return to primitive economic conditions. (Rathenau expresses such opinions, which seem justified from his point of view, in his book Nach der Flut.)[6] But this danger will be counteracted through the threefold formation of the social organism. The self-sustaining economic organism, in cooperation with the rights organism, will completely separate the monetary element from rights-oriented labor relations. Legal facilities will not have a direct influence on monetary affairs, for these are the province of the economic administration. The legal relationship between management and labor will not express itself in monetary values which, after the abolition of wages (representing the exchange relation between commodities and labor-power), will only measure commodity (and service) values. From a consideration of the social threefold formation's effect on the social organism, one must conclude that it will lead to

---

[6] Dr. Walther Rathenau. His book Nach der Flut was published in 1919. As foreign minister in Germany's post-war government, he was shot dead in the street on 24 June 1922. His books were burned by the Nazis when Hitler became chancellor.

arrangements which are not present in the political forms which have hitherto existed.

Through these arrangements, what is currently referred to as class struggle can be eliminated. This struggle results from wages being an integral part of the economic process. This book presents a social form in which the concept of wages undergoes a transformation, as does the old concept of property. Through this transformation a more viable social cooperation is made possible.

It would be superficial to think that the realization of the ideas presented here would result in time-wages being converted into piece-wages. A one-sided view could lead to this opinion. However, what is advocated here is not piece-wages, but the abolishment of the wage system in favor of a contractual sharing system in respect of the common achievements of management and labor — in conjunction, of course, with the overall structure of the social organism. To hold that the workers' share of the proceeds should consist of piece-wages is to fail to see that a contractual sharing system – in no sense a wage system – expresses the value of what has been produced in a way which changes the workers' social position in relation to the other members of society. This position is completely different from the one which arose through one-sided, economically conditioned class supremacy. The need for the elimination of the class struggle is therewith satisfied.

In socialist circles one frequently hears that evolution will supply the solution to the social question, that one cannot express opinions and then expect them to be put into practice. This must be answered as follows: Certainly evolution must supply the necessary social adjustments, but in the social organism the impulses behind human ideas are realities. When the times are more advanced and what today can only be thought is realized, only then will what has been thought be contained in evolution. However, it will then be too late to accomplish what is already demanded by today's events. It is not possible to consider evolution objectively as regards the social organism. One must activate evolution. It is therefore disastrous for sound social thinking that current opinion desires to prove social necessities in the same way that natural science proves things. Proof, as far as social conceptions are concerned, can only be attained if one's views can assimilate not only what exists now, but also what is present in human impulses as striving to be realized.

One of the effects through which the threefold formation of the social organism will prove itself to be based on the essential nature of human society is the severance of judicial activities from state institutions. It will be incumbent on the latter to establish the rights between persons or groups of persons. Judicial decisions however, will depend upon facilities formed by the spiritual organization. This judicial decision making is, to a large extent, dependent on the judge's ability to perceive and understand the defendant's situation. Such perception and understanding will be present if the confidence which men feel towards the facilities of the spiritual organization is extended to include the courts. The spiritual organization might nominate judges from the various cultural professions. After a certain length of time they would return to their own professions. Within certain limits, every person would then be able to select the nominee, for a period of five or ten years, in whom he has sufficient confidence to accept his verdict in a civil or criminal case, should one arise. To make such a selection meaningful, there would have to be enough judges available in the vicinity of each person's place of residence. A plaintiff would always be obliged to direct himself to a competent judge in the respondent's vicinity.

Just consider the importance such an arrangement would have had in the Austria-Hungarian districts. The members of each nationality in mixed-language districts could have chosen judges from their own people. Whoever is familiar with the Austrian situation will recognize what a compensatory effect such an arrangement could have had in the life of those peoples. Aside from the nationality question, there are other areas in which such arrangements can contribute to sound development. Officials selected by the spiritual organization's administration will assist the judges and courts with technical points of law, but will themselves not hold decision-making authority. Appeal courts will also be formed by this administration. An essential characteristic of such an arrangement is that a judge, because of his life outside his judgeship – which he could only hold for a limited period – can be familiar with the sensibilities and environment of the defendant. The healthy social organism will everywhere attract social understanding to its institutions, and judicial activities will be no exception. The execution of sentences is the responsibility of the rights-state.

It is not possible to enter into a description of the arrangements which would become necessary in other areas of life as the result of implementing these suggestions. Such a description would obviously require an almost unlimited amount of space.

The individual examples used will have shown that the exposition of these views does not constitute an attempt to revive the three estates – food producers, military, and philosophers – as some have mistakenly assumed upon hearing my lectures on the subject. The opposite of such a structure is intended. Human beings will not be segregated into classes or estates; the social organism itself will be appropriately formed. Through this formation man will be able to be truly man. The threefold formation will enable him to participate in all three social sectors. He will have a professional interest in the sector which includes his occupation; and he will have vital connections with the others, necessitated by the nature of their institutions. The external social organism which forms the foundation for human life will be threefold; each individual will constitute a binding element for its three sectors.

Chapter Four

International Relations Between Social Organisms

The internal formation of the healthy social organism being threefold, each of the three sectors will have an independent relation to the corresponding sector of another social organism. Economic relations between countries will exist without being directly influenced by the relations between their respective rights-states. Conversely, the relations between rights-states will develop, within certain limits, completely independent of economic relations. Through this independence of development, the relations will act upon each other in a conciliatory way in cases of conflict. The resulting complex of mutual interests among the individual social organisms will make national frontiers seem inconsequential for human coexistence.

The spiritual/cultural organizations of the various countries will be able to enter into mutual relations which derive exclusively from the common spiritual life of humanity. The self-sustaining spiritual sector, independent of the state, will develop conditions which are impossible to attain when recognition of spiritual activities is dependent on the rights-state instead of the spiritual organism's administration. In this respect there is no difference between scientific activities, which are obviously international, and other spiritual activities. A people's own language, and everything related to it, also constitutes a spiritual area. National awareness itself belongs to this area. The people of one language region do not come into unnatural conflict with the people of another if political organizations and economic power are not used to assert their cultures. Should one people's culture have a greater capability for expansion and spiritual productivity than another, then its expansion will be justified and will come about peacefully if its only means of doing so are the institutions which depend on the spiritual organism.

At the present time, the strongest opposition to a threefold social organism will come from the communities which have developed from common language and culture. This opposition must give way before the goal which the times have set and of which humanity as a whole must become increasingly aware. Mankind will perceive that each of its parts can achieve a dignified existence only if all the parts are vigorously allied among themselves. Ethnic affinities, together with other natural impulses, are the historic cause of the formation of political and economic communities.

However, the forces by means of which the various peoples grow must develop with a reciprocity which is not hampered by relations between political states and economic cooperatives. This will be achieved when the ethnic communities have implemented their social threefold formation to the extent that each of the sectors can cultivate independent relations with other social organisms.

Diversified relations are therewith established between peoples, states and economic bodies which unite all the parts of humanity so that each is sensitive to the life of the others. A league of nations arises from impulses corresponding to reality.[7] It will not need to be installed because of one-sided political considerations.

Of special significance is the fact that the social goals described here, although valid for humanity in general, can be realized by each individual social organism regardless of other countries' initial attitudes. Should a social organism be formed according to the three natural sectors, the representatives of each sector could enter into international relations with others, even if these others have not yet adopted the same forms. Those who lead the way to these forms are working for a common goal of humanity. What must be

---

[7] Reference is to the organization of this name established by the victorious allies on 28 July 1919, mostly at the initiative of President Wilson. It had no sooner been created than it suffered an almost mortal blow when the United States Congress rejected it.

accomplished is far more likely to come about on the strength of human impulses which have their roots in life, than through decisions and agreements made at congresses and the like. The thoughts which underlie these goals are based on reality; they are to be pursued in all human communities.

Whoever has followed the political events of the last decades from the point of view represented here, will have perceived how the various states, with their merged spiritual, rights and economic sectors, were approaching catastrophe in international relations. At the same time, however, he could also see that forces of a contrary nature were arising as unconscious human impulses and pointing the way toward the threefold formation. This will be the remedy for the shock caused by fanaticism for uniform statism. But the so-called 'competent leaders of humanity' were not able to see what had long since been in preparation. In the spring and early summer of 1914, one could still hear statesmen saying that peace in Europe, as far as could be humanly foreseen, was secure thanks to the efforts of governments. These 'statesmen' had no idea that their words and deeds no longer had any relation whatsoever to the real course of events. But they were the experts. Those who had been developing contrary views during the last decades, such as those expressed by the author months before the outbreak of war and, finally, to a small audience in Vienna (a larger audience would only have been derisive) were considered to be eccentric.

Words to the following effect concerning the immediate dangers were spoken: 'Today's prevalent tendencies will continue to gather momentum until they finally destroy themselves. Whoever observes society with spiritual insight sees a terrible disposition to social cancerous growths everywhere. This is cause for great concern. It is so terrible and distressing that even if a person could otherwise suppress all enthusiasm for the knowledge of life's events obtainable through a science which recognizes the spirit, he would still feel obliged to speak, to cry out to the world about the remedy. If the social organism continues to develop as it has until now, injuries to culture will occur which are to this organism what cancer is to the human physical organism.' But the views of the ruling circles, based on just such undercurrents which they refused to recognize, led them to take measures better left undone and to take none which could have instilled mutual trust among the members of the various human communities.

Whoever believes that social exigencies played no direct role as a cause of the present world catastrophe, should consider what would have become of the political impulses of those states heading for war had their statesmen taken these exigencies seriously and acted upon them. They would then not have created the inflammable conditions which eventually led to an explosion. If, during the past decades, one had observed the cancer which had grown into the relations between states as the result of the ruling circles' social conduct, one could understand how, as early as 1888, a personage of general human spiritual interests was obliged to state the following in view of how social will was being expressed in these ruling circles: 'The goal is to turn the whole of humanity into an empire of brothers who, following only the noblest of motives, stride forward in unison. Whoever follows history on the map of Europe, however, can easily believe that what the immediate future holds in store is a general mass slaughter'; and only the thought that a 'way to the true goodness of human life' must be found can maintain a sense of human dignity. This thought is one 'which does not seem to coincide with our and our neighbors' enormous war-like preparations; it is one in which I, nevertheless, believe, and which must enlighten us, unless we prefer to simply do away with human life by common consent and designate an official suicide day.' (Herman Grimm, 1888, on page 46 of his book: Fifteen Essays — The Last Five Years). What were these 'war-like preparations' but measures enacted by people who wanted to maintain the uniform state structure in spite of the fact that this form had become contradictory to the fundamentals of healthy cooperation between peoples? Such healthy cooperation could, however, be accomplished by that social organism which is based on the necessities of the times.

The Austria-Hungarian state structure had been in need of a reorganization for more than half a century.[8] Its spiritual life, with roots in a multiplicity of ethnic communities, required the development of a form for which the obsolete uniform state was a hindrance. The Serbo-Austrian conflict, which was the starting-point of the world-war catastrophe, is the most valid proof that, as of a certain time, the political borders of this uniform state should not have constituted the borders for its ethnic life as well.[9] Had the possibility existed for a self-sustaining spiritual life, independent of the political

---

[8] An American journalist-historian has since seen it this way. 'The Danube monarchy was dying of indigestion. For centuries a minority of German-Austrians had ruled over the polyglot empire of a dozen nationalities and stamped their language and culture on it. But since 1848 their hold had been weakening. The minorities could not be digested. Austria was not a melting pot. In the 1860s the Italians had broken away and in 1867 the Hungarians had won equality with the Germans under the so-called Dual Monarchy. Now, as the twentieth century began, the various Slav peoples — the Czechs, the Slovaks, the Serbs, the Croats and the others — were demanding equality and at least national autonomy. Austrian politics had become dominated by the bitter quarrel of the nationalities. But this was not all. There was social revolt too and this often transcended the racial struggle ...' William L. Shirer, *The Rise and Fall of the Third Reich*, Simon & Schuster, New York, 1960.

[9] The Austrian Grand Duke Franz Ferdinand and his wife were assassinated on 28 June 1914 in Sarajevo by members of a Serbian secret society. The assassination was the outward event which triggered the war.

state and its borders, to develop beyond these borders in harmony with the goals of the ethnic groups, then the conflict, which had its roots in the spiritual sector, would not have exploded in a political catastrophe. Development in this direction seemed completely impossible, if not outright nonsensical, to those in Austria-Hungary who imagined that their thinking was 'statesman-like.' Their thought-habits could not conceive of any other possibility but that the state borders must coincide with national communities. An understanding of the fact that spiritual organizations, including schools and other branches of spiritual life, could be established without regard to state borders was contrary to their thinking. Nevertheless, this 'unthinkable' arrangement constitutes the requirement of modern times for international relations. The practical thinker should not let himself be restrained by the seemingly impossible and believe that arrangements which satisfy this requirement would meet with insurmountable difficulties; he should rather direct his efforts toward overcoming these difficulties. Instead of bringing the 'statesmanlike' thinking into agreement with the requirements of the times, efforts were made to sustain the uniform state in opposition to these requirements. This state therefore took on an increasingly impossible structure. By the second decade of the twentieth century, it was unable to preserve itself in the old form and had the choice of awaiting dissolution or outwardly maintaining the inwardly impossible by means of the force which manifested itself in the war. The Austria-Hungarian 'statesmen' had only two choices in 1914: either to direct their efforts toward achieving the conditions necessary for a healthy social organism, and inform the world of their purpose, thereby awakening new confidence, or they had to unleash a war in order to maintain the old structure. Only by considering the events of 1914 with this background in mind can one judge the question of guilt fairly. Through the participation of many ethnic groups in its state structure, Austria-Hungary's historical mission may well have been above all to develop a healthy social organism. This mission was not recognized. It was this sin against the spirit of historical evolution that drove Austria-Hungary to war.

And the German Empire?[10] It was founded at a time when the modern requirements for a healthy social organism were striving for recognition. This recognition could have given the Empire's existence its historical justification. Social impulses were concentrated in this central European Empire as though historically predestined to live themselves out within its borders. Social thinking arose in many places, but in the German

---

[10] The 'second' German Empire was founded on 18 January 1871 through the efforts of its chancellor, Otto von Bismarck. On that date, King Wilhelm I of Prussia was proclaimed Emperor of Germany in the Hall of Mirrors at Versailles.

Empire it took a special form which indicated where it was heading. This should have supplied the Empire with a purpose. This should have shown its administrators where its mission lay. The justification for this Empire could have been contained in a modern compatibility of nations [ethnicities], had the newly-created Empire been given a purpose which coincided with the forces of history. Instead of rising to the greatness of this mission, those responsible remained at the level of social reforms corresponding to the needs of the moment, and were happy when these reforms were admired abroad.[11] At the same time they were moving toward an external power structure based on forms deriving from the most antiquated concepts about the power and splendor of states. An empire was built which, like the Austria-Hungarian state structure, contradicted the forces present in the various ethnic communities at that historic moment. The administrators of this empire saw nothing of these forces. The state structure which they had in mind could only be based on military power. The requirements of modern history would have been

---

[11] During the period 1883 to 1889 Bismarck had enacted various such reforms, which went far beyond anything known at that time in other countries. They included compulsory insurance for old-age sickness, accidents and incapacity and they were operated by the state but financed by employees and employers. Such reforms had the effect of dampening the workers' enthusiasm for extreme socialism but, at the same time, increased their faith in the state as protector.

satisfied by the implementation of the impulse for a healthy social organism. If this had been done, relations between nations would have been different in 1914. Because of their lack of understanding of modern requirements in ethnic relations, German policy had reached the zero-point in 1914 as far as possibilities for further action were concerned. During the preceding decades they had understood nothing of what should have been done, and German policy had been occupied with every possibility that had no relation to modern evolutionary forces, and therefore had to collapse like a house of cards due to its lack of content.

A true picture of the historic events surrounding the German Empire's tragic destiny would emerge if an examination were made of the decisive events in Berlin at the end of July and August 1, 1914, and the facts presented truthfully to the world.[12] Little is known of

---

[12] The memoirs of General Helmuth von Moltke, Chief of the German General Staff at the outbreak of the war, were ready for publication in May 1919. Von Moltke describes the German Government's attitude at that time, especially on 31 July and 1 August 1914:'The atmosphere grew steadily more tense and I was completely alone.' Then he was told by the Kaiser, 'So now you can do whatever you want.' Rudolf Steiner wrote in a commentary: 'So there it was: the Chief of the General Staff stood completely alone. Due to the fact that German policy had reached the zero-point, Europe's destiny on 31 July and 1 August rested in the hands of a man who was obliged to do his military duty.' (Vorbemerkungen zu Die Schuld am Krieg, Betrachtungen und Erinnerungen des Generalstabschefs H. von Moltke.) Aufsätze über die Dreigliederung des Sozialen Organismus. This 'military duty' involved implementing

these events, either in Germany or abroad. Whoever is familiar with them knows that German policy at that time was comparable to a house of cards, and because of its arrival at a zero-point of activity, the decision as to whether and how the war was to begin had to be left to the military. The responsible military authorities at that time could not, from the military viewpoint, have acted in any other way than they did, because from this viewpoint the situation could only be seen as they saw it. Outside the military sector things had come to the point where action was no longer possible. All this would emerge as historical fact if someone were to occupy himself with bringing to light the events which took place in Berlin at the end of July and the beginning of August, namely, everything which occurred on August

---

the German army's predetermined war-plan, prepared by von Moltke's predecessor General Schlieffen, which provided for the domination of France before invading Russia. France was to be attacked through Belgium and Holland. Von Moltke modified the plan to the extent that Holland was omitted. His memoirs were suppressed in 1919, but Rudolf Steiner, who was personally acquainted with him, was familiar with their contents. In an interview which appeared in the French newspaper Le Matin in October 1921,Steiner said that the memoirs should have been published in 1919, but they were suppressed because of fear on the part of the authorities. 'Why this fear? These memoirs are in no way an accusation against the imperial government. Something else is involved, which is perhaps even worse: that this imperial government found itself in a state of complete confusion and under an incredibly frivolous and ignorant leadership.' Jules Sauerman's interview with Dr. Rudolf Steiner on the unpublished memoirs of the late Chief of the German General Staff von Moltke. ibid.

1, and July 31. The illusion persists that an insight into these events would not be particularly enlightening if one is familiar with the events which led up to this time. It is not possible, however, to discuss the 'guilt question' without this insight. Certainly one may have knowledge through other means of the causes which were long present; but insight shows how these causes acted on events.

The concepts which at that time drove Germany's leaders to war continued their ruinous work. They became the national sentiment. They prevented those in power from developing the necessary insight through the bitter experience of these last terrible years. Wishing to take advantage of the receptivity which might have resulted from this experience, I attempted to make known during the war, which I considered to be the most suitable time, the basic concept of a healthy social organism and its consequences for German policy, to personages in Germany and Austria whose influence could still have been brought to bear in furthering these impulse.[13] Those persons who honestly had the German

---

[13] Steiner wrote a memorandum directed to leading government circles in Germany and Austria which contained his ideas concerning the way these countries could act in a manner which would have been beneficial to themselves and the world. Count Otto Lerchenfeld brought a memorandum to the German state secretary Kuhlman among others, and Count Ludwig Polzer-Hoditz to his brother, Austria's chief cabinet officer. The memoranda were not

people's destiny at heart participated in the attempt to gain a hearing for these ideas. But the attempt was futile. The habits of thinking resisted such impulses which, to the military mentality, appeared unworkable. 'Separation of church and school': yes, that would be something; but they got no further. The thoughts of the 'statesman-like' thinkers had long been running along the same track, and more drastic measures were beyond them. Well-meaning people suggested that I make these ideas public. This was most unsuitable advice at the time. What good could it have done to have these ideas, among so many others, and coming from a private individual, disseminated. It is in the nature of these impulses that they could only have been influential, at that time if they had come from the appropriate places. Had the sense of these impulses been favorably proclaimed from the right quarters, the peoples of central Europe would have realized that here is something which coincides with their more or less conscious desires. And the Russian peoples in the east would surely have been sympathetic to these impulses as an alternative to czarism. This can only be denied by someone who has no feeling for the receptivity of the East-European mind for healthy social ideas. Instead of

---

published during Steiner's lifetime. They are included in *Aufsätze über die Dreigliederung des Sozialen Organismus.*

a pronouncement of such ideas, however, came Brest-Litovsk.[14]

That military thinking could not avert the catastrophe in central and eastern Europe was apparent to all but the military minds. The cause of the German people's misfortune was unwillingness to see that the catastrophe was unavoidable. Nobody wanted to believe that there was no sense of historic necessity in the places where decisions were being made. Whoever knew something of these necessities also realized that there were personages among the English-speaking peoples who understood the forces at work in the peoples of central and eastern Europe. They were convinced that a situation was brewing which must result in mighty social upheavals – but only in central and eastern Europe, for it was felt that there was not yet either a historical necessity or a possibility for such upheavals in the English-speaking world. Policy was

---

[14] On 15 December 1917. the peace treaty between Germany and Russia was signed at Brest-Litovsk. The conditions imposed by Germany were extremely hard (very comparable to those imposed on her by the allies a year later). As a result of this accord, Germany was free to concentrate its troops in the west. In Russia, only two months after the revolution, the new communist government led by Lenin was anxious to consolidate its power at home without having to continue the inherited war. The suspicion also exists that Lenin had secretly agreed to make peace with Germany while he was still in exile in Switzerland, in return for his famous trip from Zürich to Russia through Germany in a sealed railway carriage, in order to take command of the revolution.

formulated accordingly. This was not understood in central and eastern Europe, and policy was formulated in such a way that it had to collapse like a house of cards. The only effective policy would have been one based on an insight into the English-speaking world's liberal recognition of historical necessities. But the 'diplomats' would have found a suggestion for such a policy superfluous.

Instead of such a policy, which could have been very advantageous for central and eastern Europe before the catastrophe of war overtook it, they continued in the same old diplomatic rut in spite of the liberal orientation of English policy. Furthermore, during the horrors of war they did not learn from bitter experience that the mission presented to the world in political declarations from America should be countered by one born of the vital forces of Europe. An understanding could have been reached between the mission presented by Woodrow Wilson from the American point of view, and one heard over the thunder of cannons as a European spiritual impulse. Any other talk of an understanding rang hollow in view of the historical necessities.

But a sense of mission based on modern humanity's true needs was lacking in those responsible for the German empire's policy. Therefore, what the autumn of 1918 brought was inevitable. The collapse of military power was accompanied by a spiritual capitulation.

Instead of exerting European will at that time in an attempt to assert the German people's spiritual impulses, came the simple submission to Wilson's fourteen point. [15] Wilson was confronted with a Germany which had nothing to say for itself. Whatever Wilson may think about his own fourteen points, he could only help Germany to fulfill what the country itself wills. Surely he must have expected a demonstration of this desire. But to the nullity of German policy at the beginning of the war was added the nullity of 1918; the terrible spiritual capitulation came, brought on by a man

---

[15] President Wilson's 'fourteen points' constituted the ideological basis for the principle of 'self-determination of peoples,' which was to underlie the political restructuring of Europe after the war. This principle presupposes that ethnic groups (peoples, nations) are perfectly separable and definable, like so many individual pieces of a jigsaw puzzle. If each governs itself through its own national state, then the cause of political morality is served. In fact, Europe was and is a quilt of nations with many overlapping ethnic gray regions. The effect of self-determination or the 'nationalities principle' is the disenfranchisement of many smaller or larger minorities with the resultant bitterness and frustration. The course of history since this principle was put into effect in Europe and elsewhere would seem to support such criticism. Winston Churchill wrote the following about the carving up of the Austria-Hungarian empire: 'The second cardinal tragedy was the complete break-up of the Austria-Hungarian Empire ... There is not one of these peoples or provinces that constituted the Empire of the Hapsburgs to whom gaining their independence has not brought the tortures which ancient poets and theologians had reserved for the damned.' *The Second World War, Vol. 1, Chap. i, The Gathering Storm.* According to the idea of the 'social triformation,' or 'threefold society,' the nationalities (ethnic) problem can only be solved by liberating 'national' life from the power of the political state. In other words, the creation of a free cultural-spiritual sector.

in whom many in the German lands had placed something like a last hope.

Lack of faith in insights derived from historically active forces; unwillingness to recognize knowledge derived from spiritually related impulses: this was what produced central Europe's situation. Now a new situation has been created by the catastrophe of war. It can be characterized by the idea of humanity's social impulses as it has been interpreted in this book. These social impulses speak a language which confronts the whole civilized world with a mission. Shall thinking about what must now come about in respect of the social question reach the same zero-point as did central European policy in respect of its mission in 1914? Countries which were able to remain aloof from the events of that time may not do so as far as the social movement is concerned. In this question there should be no political opponents and no neutrals; there should only be one humanity, working together, which is able to read the signs of the times and act in accordance with them.

The intentions described in this book make it possible to understand why the appeal 'To the German People and the Civilized World,' which is reproduced in the following chapter, was formulated by the author some time ago and communicated to the world — especially to the peoples of central Europe — by a committee which sympathized with its aims. The present situation is different from the one prevalent at the time in which it was communicated to relatively few. At that time a wider propagation would have been considered 'literature.' Today the public must bring to it what it could not have brought a short time ago: understanding men and women who want to work for what it advocates if it is worth being understood and being put into practice. What should come about now is only possible through the activity of such people.

Appendix

To the German People and the Civilized World[16]

The German people believed that its imperial structure, erected half a century ago, would last for an unlimited time. In August 1914, they felt that the imminent catastrophe of war would prove this structure invincible. Today only its ruins are left. After such an experience retrospection is in order, for this experience has proved the opinions of half a century, especially the dominant thoughts of the war years, to be tragically erroneous. What are the reasons behind this erroneous thinking? This question must induce retrospection in the minds of the German people. Its potentiality for life depends on whether the strength exists for this kind of self-examination. Its future depends on whether it can earnestly ask the following question: how did we fall into error? If the German people asks itself this question today, it will realize that it established an Empire half a

---

[16] To the German People and the Civilized World. This appeal was counter-signed by a number of personages from Germany, Austria and Switzerland. Probably the only one immediately recognizable in the English-speaking world of today is Hermann Hesse. It was printed and distributed by committees in these and other European countries.

century ago but omitted to assign to this Empire the mission which corresponds to the inner essence of its people.

The Empire was established. At first it was occupied with bringing its inner life into harmony with the requirements of tradition and the new needs which developed from year to year. Later, efforts were directed toward consolidating and enlarging the outward power structure, which was based on material strength. At the same time means were employed which were directed at the social demands of the day, in some cases appropriate to the needs, but which lacked the larger goal which should have resulted from knowledge of the evolutionary forces to which mankind must direct itself. Therefore, the Empire was placed in the world without a substantial goal to justify its existence. The war-catastrophe revealed this fact in a tragic way. Previous to the war's outbreak, those in the non-German world could see nothing in the conduct of the Empire's affairs which could lead them to think that its authorities were fulfilling a historic mission that should not be swept away. The fact that these authorities did not encounter such a mission necessarily engendered an attitude in the non-German world which was, to one who has a real insight, the more profound reason for the German downfall.

A very great deal depends upon the German people's objective discernment of this fact. The insight which has remained hidden for the past fifty years should emerge during these calamitous times. In place of trivial thinking about immediate requirements, a broader view of life should now appear, which strives with powerful thinking to recognize modern humanity's evolutionary forces and is courageously dedicated to them. The petty attempts to neutralize all those who pay heed to these evolutionary forces must cease. The arrogance and superciliousness of those who imagine themselves to be practical, but whose practicality is the disguised narrow-mindedness which has in fact induced the calamity, must cease. Attention should be paid to what those who are decried as idealists, but who in reality are the practical ones, have to say about the evolutionary needs of modern times.

'Practical' people of every persuasion have seen the advent of new human demands for a long time. But they wanted to deal with these demands within the framework of the old traditional thinking and institutions. Modern economic life has produced these demands. To satisfy them by means of private initiative seemed impossible. The transfer of private enterprise to community enterprise in some cases appeared necessary to a certain class of people; and this was carried out where they thought it was useful. Radical transfer of all individual enterprise to community enterprise was the goal of another class which was not interested in retaining the customary private objectives in the new economy.

All the efforts relating to the new requirements which have been made until now have one thing in common. They strive toward the socialization of the private sector and reckon with it being taken over by the communities (states, municipalities), which have developed from conditions which have nothing to do with present requirements. Or, they reckon with newer kinds of communities (cooperatives, for example), which are not fully in harmony with these new requirements, having been copied from the old forms using traditional thought-habits.

The truth is that no form of community which corresponds to these old thought-habits can cope with such requirements. The forces of the times are pressing for knowledge of a social structure for humanity which is completely different from what is commonly envisaged. Social communities hitherto have, for the most part, been formed by human instinct. To penetrate their forces with full consciousness is a mission of the times.

The social organism is formed like the natural organism. As the natural organism must provide for thinking by means of the head and not the lungs, the formation of the social organism in systems, none of which can assume the functions of the others, although each must cooperate with the others while always maintaining its autonomy, is necessary.

The economy can prosper only if it develops, as an autonomous member of the social organism, according to its own forces and laws, and if it does not introduce confusion into its structure by letting itself be drained by another member of the social organism, the political one. This politically active member must function, fully autonomous, alongside the economy, as the respiratory system functions alongside the head system in the natural organism. Healthy cooperation cannot be attained by means of a single legislative and administrative organ, but by each system having its own mutually cooperating legislature and administration. The political system, by absorbing the economy, inevitably destroys it; and the economic system loses its vital force when it becomes political.

A third member of the social organism, in full autonomy and formed from its own potentialities, must be added to these two: that of spiritual production, to which the spiritual parts of the other two sectors, supplied to them by this third sector, belong. It must have its own legitimate rules and administration and not be administered or influenced by the other two, except in the sense that the members of the natural organism mutually influence each other.

Already today one can scientifically substantiate and develop in detail what has been said here about the social organism's needs. In this presentation only a general indication can be given for all those who wish to pursue them.

The German Empire was founded at a time when these needs were converging on mankind. Its administrators did not understand the need for setting the Empire's mission accordingly. A view to these necessities would not only have given the Empire the correct inner structure; it would also have lent justification to its foreign policy. The German people could have lived together with the non-German peoples through such a policy.

Insight should now mature from the calamity. One should develop a will for the best possible social organism. Not a Germany which no longer exists should face the world, but a spiritual, a political and an economic system should propose to deal as autonomous delegations, through their representatives, with those who crushed that Germany which became an impossible social structure due to the confusion of its three systems.

One can anticipate the experts who object to the complexity of these suggestions and find it uncomfortable even to think about three systems cooperating with each other, because they wish to know nothing of the real requirements of life and would structure everything according to the comfortable requirements of their thinking. This must become clear to them: either people will accommodate their thinking to the requirements of reality, or they will have learned nothing from the calamity and will cause innumerable new ones to occur in the future.

Rudolf Steiner

About the Author

Rudolf Steiner was born in the town of Kraljevic, then in the Austrian-Hungarian Empire, later in Yugoslavia, now in Croacia, on February 27, 1861, and died in Dornach, Switzerland, on March 30, 1925. He was a scientist, writer, lecturer and philosopher, as well as being the founder and leading light of Anthroposophy, a movement based on the belief that there is a spiritual world comprehensible to pure thought but accessible only to the highest faculties of mental (spiritual) activity.

Steiner edited Goethe's scientific works, and from 1889 to 1896 worked on the standard version of his complete works at Weimer. During this period, he wrote his "Philosophy of Freedom," then moved to Berlin to edit the literary journal "Magazin für Literatur" and to begin an extensive, life-long lecturing career.

Convinced of the possibility of spiritual perception independent of the senses, he called the activity of his research "Anthroposophy," centering on "knowledge produced by the higher self in man." All of his many books and over 6,000 lectures are available in German and most in English as well.

The practical results of Steiner's work include many Waldorf schools the world over, bio-dynamic agriculture and anthroposophical medicine. These movements continue growing and nourishing society.

END

About the Translator

Frank Thomas Smith is an American expatriate originally from Brooklyn, New York. Working in the international airline business, he has lived most of his life abroad, in Europe and South America. He has moonlighted in consulting, education (Waldorf) and writing. He is the editor and publisher of the,

www.SouthernCrossReview.org.

Contact: fts@SouthernCrossReview.org

On-line Activities

What is Anthroposophy?

Rudolf Steiner described Anthroposophy as a path of knowledge to guide the spiritual in the human being to the spiritual in the cosmos. It manifests as a necessity of the heart and feeling. It is for those who feel that certain questions about the nature of man and the world are basic necessities of life, like hunger and thirst. He was a clairvoyant who spoke from his direct cognition of the spiritual world. However, he did not see his work as a religion or as sectarian, but rather sought to found a universal 'science of the spirit.' A fundamental aspect of Anthroposophy is the recognition of a real spiritual world in addition to the visible physical one.

All of Rudolf Steiner's books and thousands of lectures which have been translated into English are available free of charge at the Rudolf Steiner Archive & e.Lib.

Visit the author's www.SouthernCrossReview.org **e.Zine**

Visit the Rudolf Steiner Archive & e.Lib, www.RSArchive.org.

www.ingramcontent.com/pod-product-compliance
Lightning Source LLC
Chambersburg PA
CBHW050123280326
41933CB00010B/1217